FREE SPACE

A R C H I T E C T U R E

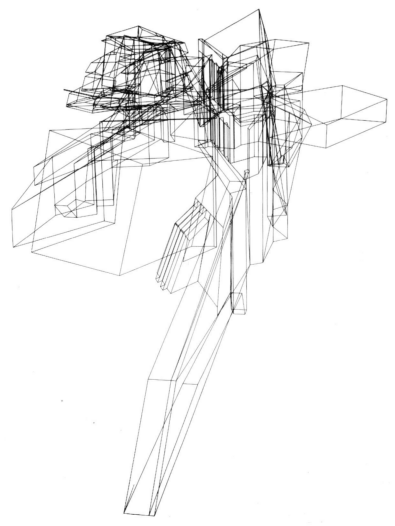

GÜNTHER DOMENIG, STEINHAUS, OSSIACHERSEE, CARINTHIA

Architectural Design

Edited by Andreas C Papadakis

FREE SPACE
A R C H I T E C T U R E

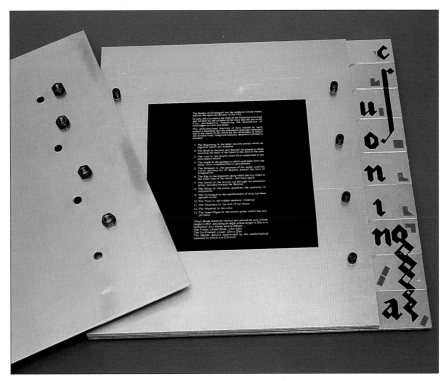

OPPOSITE: JOHN HEJDUK, *BOOK G*;
ABOVE: DANIEL LIBESKIND, MASTERPLAN; FROM *THE BOOKS OF GRONINGEN*. A PROJECT TO CELEBRATE 950 YEARS OF
GRONINGEN WHICH IS FEATURED IN THE ISSUE OF *ART & DESIGN* 1/2 92, VOL 25, 'MARKING THE CITY BOUNDARIES'

ACADEMY EDITIONS • LONDON

Acknowledgements

We are grateful to Sir Roger de Grey, President of the Royal Academy of Arts, for his encouragement and support; to MaryAnne Stevens, joint organiser of the Academy Forum on *The Venice Biennale and the Architecture of Pluralism*; to the many participants of the Forum and Symposium for responding with enthusiasm and at such short notice and for allowing us to reproduce their contributions in this issue.

Front Cover: Zaha Hadid, Media Park, Dusseldorf; *Back Cover*: Lebbeus Woods, Paris in the Air; *Inside Front Covers*: Toyo Ito, *Dreams* from *A Vision of Japan* exhibition at the Victoria and Albert Museum, London

Photographic Credits
p6: Kijuro Yahagi
Zaha Hadid, Media Park, Dusseldorf, and Vitra Fire Station: Edward Woodman (modelmaker: Daniel Chadwick)
All photographs for *Critical Intentions in Pluralistic Japanese Architecture*: Botond Bognar

EDITOR
Dr Andreas C Papadakis

CONSULTANTS: Catherine Cooke, Terry Farrell, Kenneth Frampton, Charles Jencks
Heinrich Klotz, Leon Krier, Robert Maxwell, Demetri Porphyrios, Kenneth Powell, Colin Rowe, Derek Walker
EDITORIAL TEAM: Maggie Toy (House Editor), Vivian Constantinopoulos, Nicola Hodges, Helen Castle
DESIGN TEAM: Andrea Bettella (Senior Designer), Mario Bettella, Sharon Anthony, Owen Thomas
SUBSCRIPTIONS MANAGER: Mira Joka BUSINESS MANAGER: Sheila de Vallée

First published in Great Britain in 1992 by *Architectural Design* an imprint of the
ACADEMY GROUP LTD, 42 LEINSTER GARDENS, LONDON W2 3AN

ISBN: 1-85490-127-3 (UK)

Architectural Design Profile 96 is published as part of *Architectural Design* Vol 62 3-4 /1992
Architectural Design Magazine is published six times a year and is available by subscription

Published in the United States of America by
ST MARTIN'S PRESS, 175 FIFTH AVENUE, NEW YORK 10010
ISBN: 0-312-07897-8 (USA)

Printed and bound in Singapore

Contents

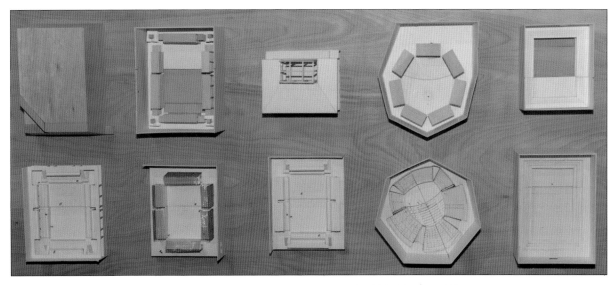

FRANK GEHRY, MODELS ON DISPLAY AT THE VENICE BIENNALE, US PAVILION

ARCHITECTURAL DESIGN PROFILE No 96
FREE SPACE ARCHITECTURE

FREEDOM AND FUNCTION

The conscious rebirth of the art of architecture is a momentous event – not achieved without a good deal of heart-searching, confusion and sheer mayhem – and world architecture now finds itself in a period of experiment, invention and, above all, freedom. Architecture can no longer be forced back into a single mould, nor should it be. The 1990s promise to be the most exciting era for architecture since the birth of the Modern Movement.

It is all the more melancholy, therefore, that so many of the players in this drama fail to understand their own parts or those of others. Modernists and Classicists can wallow in a degree of moral righteousness and social conscience, reproving the Post-Modernists and the Deconstructivists for their supposed lack of such virtues. An architect like Lebbeus Woods invites almost general disapproval, since his architecture seems to lack a message, a motive. The Free Form City might be a dream – or a nightmare – but it is an intoxicating vision for all that. Woods' ultimate concern is with the cultural regeneration of society, and it would be hard to describe his architecture as socially irrelevant. Yet it infuriates those who, like Rob Krier, see the city in terms of hierarchy and order and is all the more infuriating because such work is now being built.

Krier dismisses architectural pluralism as 'absolutely not worth talking about', irrelevant to the work of an architect. Instead, he argues for quality as the prime objective. James Stirling's attack on labelling may at first seem welcome; yet there is a negative aspect to this stance. However much the labelling process may actually blur our understanding of some buildings – is his own Staatsgalerie really 'Post-Modernist', for example? – it is a helpful tool in spreading a basic understanding of the dynamism of modern architecture to a wider public. Discussion and debate have been the foundations of increased public interest and of the emergence of architecture as an art. The much abused 'isms' are rather more than a convenience for lazy critics . . .

The Post-Modernist interlude revived the issue of style in architecture, supposedly dead since the triumph of Modernism, and renewed public interest on the basis of its concern for decoration, expression, referentiality, and appropriateness. But its virtues were skin deep and it has been subsumed in the general architectural renaissance. This is powered not so much by stylistic innovation – which can only go so far before it becomes repetitive and stale – but by a new interest in theory and ideas and in their translation into built form. Deconstruction has been a catalyst here. Philip Johnson declared three years ago that deconstruction was not a style – 'we arrogate to its

development none of the Messianic fervour of the Modern Movement, none of the exclusivity of that Catholic and Calvinist cause' . . . He saw it rather as contributing to a climate where innovation could flourish. The work of two of the architects featured in the 1988 MOMA show – Frank Gehry and Bernard Tschumi – illustrates the range of invention possible when the barriers are pushed aside.

The work of Zaha Hadid, like that of Tschumi, Eisenman or Libeskind, *exists* as much on paper as in 3D form – as such, it is a commodity of the mind, a reinforcement of the notion that the new architecture is about ideas just as much as visual forms. Itsuko Hasegawa speaks of a new architecture which 'allows us to hear the mysterious music of the universe and the rich, yet by no means transparent, world of emotions that have been disregarded by modern rationalism.'

The contemporary Japanese scene contains, as Botond Bognar emphasises, a richness within its own boundaries. Japan provides a startling contradiction to the idea that pluralism means compromise, consensus, the curbing of extremes in favour of middle-of-the-road mediocrity. If there is a formal core to contemporary Japanese architecture it lies with Isozaki's monumentalism and Ando's solemnity, but beyond this lie *inter alia* Hasegawa, Ito, Ishii, Mozuna and of course the intriguing figure of Kisho Kurokawa. Japan's pluralism is about something more than 'peaceful co-existence' – rather it is about a culture which is the forcing ground for diversity.

At the centre of the new architecture is a fascination with form and space. The tyranny of the right angle has been abolished; indeed, the tyranny of all immutable geometries is at an end. Lebbeus Woods expresses his interest in 'the secret life of the city' by his radical, 'meaningless' interventions. 'Freedom' means not just lack of sylistic constraints but a questioning of the constraints imposed by function and structure. Deconstruction, sometimes characterised as a passing fad, was a vital step in this direction.

Freedom means an architecture at one with nature – how strongly this concern emerges, for example, in the work of Hasegawa! The new Free Space architecture adapts natural forms, works with nature, utilises natural forces, questions the dominance of machines, humanistically focuses on the needs of mankind.

Architecture is not destined to a ceaseless process of fragmentation. Gradually, a new way of designing is emerging beneath the confusion of voices. The new age of freedom has already dawned for world architecture and it cannot be frozen out of existence.   *ACP / KP*

High-rise buildings in Shinjuku, Tokyo, from the exhibition Visions of Japan *at the Victoria and Albert Museum, London*

ACADEMY FORUM

THE VENICE BIENNALE, PLURALISM AND FREE SPACE ARCHITECTURE

Academy International Forum

The Royal Academy of Arts, Large South Room, London. Saturday 28th September.

The International Forum on the Venice Biennale and the Architecture of Pluralism.

Introduction by Geoffrey Broadbent

This Symposium was triggered by Andreas Papadakis and other Academy Forum members' visit to the Venice Biennale of 1991, as a result of which he threw at us a very rich mix of ideas. He invited some 50 participants, six of whom were to give slide presentations: Francesco Dal Co, who had truly master-minded the Biennale itself, and James Stirling who had earned a prestigious *A Masieri* Prize not only for his Biennale Bookshop, but also for his whole distinguished career. In addition, there was Jeremy Dixon who, with Ed Jones, had won the international 'Gateway to Venice' competition; Rob Krier who'd exhibited in the Austrian Pavilion; Lebbeus Woods, a deconstructor of Archigram-like forms; and Botond Bognar, an overwhelmed and overwhelming reporter of the current amazing scene in Japan.

Collectively, we were about as Pluralist as architects can be these days – especially if you add Robert Adam, a Classicist, and the *Architectural Design* policy of a pluralist ideology. What's more, anyone who went to the Biennale could see the work of architects – and students – of many persuasions. In the British pavilion alone there were three different styles. Therefore, it is hardly surprising that in this International Symposium, different people have spoken of Pluralism in different ways. What is the point of such a concept if they couldn't? Some thought it was merely a critics' attempt to coin a new -ism, like Classicism, Modernism and so on. Paul Finch saw Pluralism as a peaceful coexistence between different schools, different styles, different architectural movements, but others argued that if there were such a coexistence, it was by no means peaceful. 'Pluralism' as I see it, is a kind of Maoist 'let a hundred flowers bloom' provided that we know which flowers to prune, which to leave on the plant, which to take into the house and which to root out so they never bloom again. But, unlike Mao, I never encouraged blooms for the sheer sadistic pleasure of cutting some of them down. On the contrary, if a student pursues a line I dislike and proves me wrong, shows me a new architectural richness I never expected, then 'Pluralism' is working as I hoped it would. But if the 'flowers' fail my range of pragmatic tests, and gets them badly out of balance, then I'm glad they bloomed – all part of life's rich pattern – but I'm happy also that they should be cut down.

In the event, it was left to the closing remarks by Peter Cook and, above all, the presentation by Lebbeus Woods, to give this issue its name.

Forum discussion

Chairman Paul Finch, Editor of *Building Design*: This is the fourth in a series of Academy Forum discussions and the second this year to be organised in conjunction with the Royal Academy of Arts. The Academy Forum is a loose-knit organisation of journalists, architects and critics that mount symposia and exhibitions which explore new directions in art and architecture courtesy of the Academy Group. The first thing that occurred to me about the subjectmatter was what changes there have been in London in recent years which allow, for example, a master-planner to work with a

Fourth International ArchitectureForum

Venice Biennale poster

Paul Finch

Francesco Dal Co

Massimo Scolari, Glider

Aldo Rossi, design for the entrance to the Giardini

team of Modernists doing a business park in Chiswick and the same master-planner to work with a group of Classical architects designing an office development next to St Paul's. I would like to ask Francesco Dal Co to begin by commenting on his Biennale, which was a remarkable organisational success and the most significant architectural exhibition Europe has seen for a long time.

Francesco Dal Co, President of the Venice Biennale Architecture section: I don't think that the success of the Biennale is my success, it was a success of the countries that decided for the first time to participate in the Biennale. For the first time there was a real Biennale of architecture. This is not something that I did, but is something which came through the general culture, the architectural culture of the world. It is always very difficult to do a very successful exhibition of architecture because architecture is something which is only really possible to see when built.

The Biennale is an old lady of 100 years and is run by a typical Italian institution, a board of administrators consisting of representatives of trade unions and, speaking of Pluralism, they represent all the political parties in Italy. They have only one common characteristic; they know absolutely nothing about architecture. The Biennale is organised in five sectors: cinema each year, art every two years, music sometimes, theatre sometimes but architecture never. This is the scale of values in the mind of 19 members of the board of administration. The cinema is extremely important for them because for a member of a trade union to have a chance to go to the cinema every evening and sit next to Harrison Ford, or someone like that, is very exciting. Also, the Biennale traditionally pays for the members of the board to have a beautiful 15-day vacation during the cinema festival, in one of the fanciest hotels in the city.

The architectural section of the Biennale arrived only 16 years ago. The first architectural exhibition was run by Vittorio Gregotti, followed by Paolo Portoghesi, with whom I worked at that time. For the first time we succeeded in opening the Corderie de l'Arsenale with the exhibition of the facades. After that came Aldo Rossi and then I arrived as the fourth director. To give you an idea of the problems involved, the cinema festival has 450 people working for it whereas the entire architectural Biennale has only three. The cinema palace is losing gigantic quantities of money whilst the architectural exhibition made a profit this year because for the first time we succeeded in having the same number of visitors as the Exhibition of Visual Arts.

The Biennale has a great tradition bound by 23 countries who own national pavilions in the Gardens and there are 23 Commissioners whose duty it is to organise the Visual Arts Biennale. Usually these Commissioners are only interested in visual art except when they are extremely gifted like the English, Austrian or Finnish commissioners.

A year ago I organised a meeting for all the Commissioners and suddenly some of them said 'yes, it is a good idea to do a Biennale of architecture – let's do it'. 15 days before the Biennale we were still receiving requests to participate in it and there was no more room. Some important countries never made a decision. This is the reason why there is an exhibition of Tessenow in the German pavilion – because they never decided whether or not to participate. It only happened because a friend of mine, Vittorio Magnago Lampugnani, was working with me and he suggested a Tessenow exhibition.

The most typical of all the situations of the Biennale is the story of the US Pavilion, which is the only very well-established pavilion, full of air-conditioning, all the comforts and so on, owned by the Guggenheim Foundation. When I called them they said, 'It's a beautiful idea to have an exhibition, but we don't have a penny'. I thought it would be terrible if America was not in the Biennale but I had a brilliant idea, I gave Philip Johnson a call and he said 'I'll arrange the exhibition, but only if I am the Commissioner'. I didn't have the power to nominate anybody as Commissioner, but I said 'yes' and so the Americans arrived. Philip decided to select two architects in whom he was interested.

We put a great emphasis on building, on organising real competitions, on involving the public administration in financing the competition around new buildings built in the future. Two competitions were organised. The first was to redesign the main building of the Biennale, which is the Italian Pavilion, with the idea of transforming the garden complex of the Biennale into a small permanent museum of architecture. The architects who designed the pavilions are very famous ones including Rietveld, Hoffman, Scarpa and Peichl. We were thinking that this little area should work the entire year around, not only two months, and to do this we wanted to build the first *kunsthalle* of Venice, the first real museum in the city which could broaden its possibilities for cultural activity. The second thing was to transform the old cinema palace, where the festival of cinema takes place, into a modern structure so that it could be used as a congress hall during the rest of the year. Of these two competitions, one was reserved for Italians and one for both foreigners and Italians. The latter was won by Rafael Moneo.

The US Pavilion

Another project we started was that of creating a gate for the entrance to the gardens because the gardens are not protected. It is a big social problem because during the winter, people get inside the pavilions and do a lot of damage. Aldo Rossi designed what we could call a Neo-Fascist entrance using Fascist revolutionary lettering. Unfortunately the building was never built because of the authority of the Italian administration; they said that they wanted this building but they never gave their permission. The building was only represented on the poster of the exhibition. We needed to do something provocative so we said to my friend Massimo Scolari, 'OK, Massimo, do something very big'. And so he did! It is a huge symbolic glider placed in front of the Arsenale of Venice; the Corderie is behind it. This glider was very successful and there are some people who say they want to keep the glider there forever, but unfortunately we didn't have the funds to build it in materials that would resist a winter. We had a programme to build four buildings and we succeeded only in building a sculpture and one building because of the shortage of money. We had not been able to build the new gate of the gardens which was designed by Aldo Rossi, so we put all our energy into building James Stirling's new bookshop and Massimo Scolari's great sculpture. How this fits into the topic of discussion today I think is very clear: it's impossible to do a Biennale which is not Pluralistic.

Poster for the development of the Lido Cinema Competition

If you have more than 30 countries participating, the fact that they are as different as England and Greece, or Austria and Romania, implies the idea of Pluralism. My impression of what came out of this Biennale is that many of the critical categories or labels we used in the past to give a meaning to the multiplicity of architectural culture are no longer able to express the multiplicity of events which are going on in architecture. If we examine the architecture of the world not just through the glasses of our magazines or our cultural media, but the centre where the architectural culture is worked out, and we examine the phenomenon semantically, I think that Pluralism is by itself an expression which can qualify as a natural architecture. I think that the contribution of the Biennale is to enlarge the view, to examine the architecture in the world and see it not just as a by-product of London, Paris, New York and Los Angeles. It is a great source of pride for the Biennale to have been able to erect a building of one of the great architects of our age, after a century in which it was nearly impossible to put a new store in the centre of Venice.

In the Corderie we put the great masters Aldo Rossi, Rafael Moneo and James Stirling into an exhibition of the competition for the new cinema palace and after that more than 200 metres of the Corderie were given over to the schools. The Corderie is a magnificent space 330-metres long, each one of the spaces between the columns is 6 x 6 x 6 metres and was devoted to one of the schools. We invited 43 schools from all over the world and we told them they had this space and should arrange an exhibition which gives an idea of what they are and what they're doing. What is beautiful is the fact that the students came together from all over the world to work there in the way they wanted to. Obviously there was a gigantic fight because they all wanted to invade each other's space, but afterwards they organised a party and there were no more disagreements among the students.

Fumihiko Maki, Lido Cinema Competition entry

The Director of the Biennale has no power or responsibility for what is exhibited inside the pavilions, this is the responsibility of the Commissioners. An exhibition which I liked very much was that of the architect Dimitri Pikionis in the Greek Pavilion. In my opinion, he was a very important character who started working during the 1930s and developed beautiful work as the architect responsible for the layout of the Acropolis in Athens. He is an architect

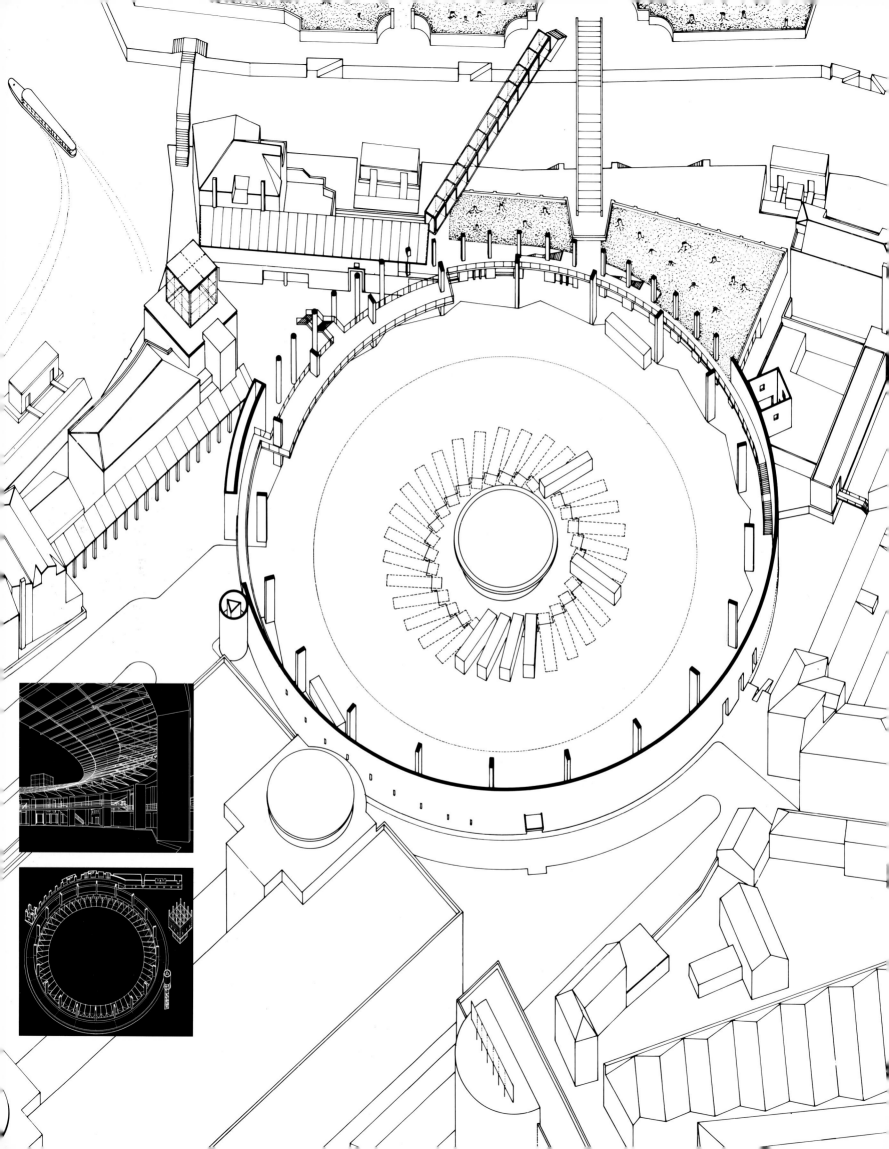

everybody knows because everybody walks on his building without recognising his work. This is an expression of incredible taste which is also confirmed by the work he did as a free architect during both the 1930s and 50s.

Jeremy Dixon and Ed Jones, 'Gateway to Venice' competition entry

Jeremy Dixon, partner with Ed Jones, of BDP: Our entry to the Biennale competition is called both a 'Gateway to Venice' and 'the Bus Station', two rather contradictory labels, but they suggest the way in which the competition was set; to have an urban idea that might be important to Venice, a practical problem that needs solving.

The location of our project is next to the railway station, where the Grand Canal turns the corner and becomes part of the industrial landscape of Venice. Arriving at Venice is quite a drama, whether you come by air, road, or train, the whole thrill of Venice is the way in which you're dramatically taken off modern transport systems and put on to the boats and footpaths. One of the things we found ourselves comparing was the nature of arrival by train which is essentially in straight lines, and with the arrival by car or bus which is freer and can take a more generous and easy-going course. We were interested in the kind of movement that the buses made as they approached Venice and the question of how people actually move in Venice itself. The circle has the characteristic of implied radial geometry away from the centre, which fits into this notion that the people who are coming to Venice are not wanting to get onto the Grand Canal, they want to get out into the town through the small paths.

Jeremy Dixon

This circular solution looks at the problem of parking buses, coming in, dropping off and picking up people. There's also a turn-around time for almost half an hour where the bus drivers rest. In the middle of the circle is a place for the drivers' coffee, in the middle of that is their washroom, and in the middle of that is a little wash-basin, so there's a kind of gradual particularisation of privacy towards the middle of the circle. The circle is therefore functional, and one could justify it as quite reasonable in terms of the workings of a bus station. However, the way in which this building dominates the scene is a formal problem for which one had to make some proposition; what we are saying is that the building is neither a circular object nor simply a circus as an interior. It's a partly disclosed circular exterior which allows a clear space to exist within which isn't over-ruled by the scale of the surrounding car-park buildings.

Henry Meyric Hughes, Head of Visual Arts, The British Council, and Commissioner for the British Pavilion: On 27th November, the foreign commissioners who were responsible for the 30 national pavilions in the Giardini were summoned to a meeting with Francesco Dal Co. He put to us a terrifying proposition for the representatives of those countries who had no budgets for the current year: that we should put together a major exhibition in our pavilions in the space of six months to fit in with all his own very exciting projects, both for the Corderie of the art schools and the different architectural competitions. Happily there was among us one very distinguished foreign commissioner, Hans Hollein, who persuaded a number of us, including me, that it was possible in the time available.

Jeremy Dixon and Ed Jones, 'Gateway to Venice', model

One reason I think we decided to do it, and to do it so whole-heartedly, was perhaps the recognition that in Italy there is a visual arts culture which is much more developed and less compartmentalised than in Britain. We thought we would try to put together a succession of rooms in our own pavilion which would relate to each other but which would above all be pleasurable to the visitor. I hope to a greater or lesser extent that we succeeded in this, but certainly it wasn't the conventional kind of architectural exhibition which is put on for architects only. In the front room, there were selected drawings by James Stirling; leading into Norman Foster's room, there were photographs taken by Ben Johnson of some of Foster's projects – very much an artist's interpretation or re-interpretation of an architectural project. Going on from there, we had a room with some extraordinarily colourful collages by John Outram of buildings which looked as if they had come out of some science-fiction manual. Facing onto the Giardini at the back were photographs by Michael Hopkins, not on the walls at all, but on slanted panels on the ceiling so those who had already got tired could lie on the bench beneath and look up at pictures of cricket in Lords cricket ground. Moving on from there was a spectacular model from Nick Grimshaw created especially for the Biennale, and we of course were

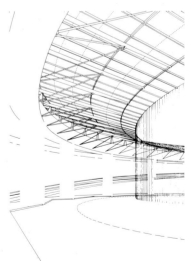

Jeremy Dixon and Ed Jones, 'Gateway to Venice', axonometric

Edwina Sassoon and Henry Meyric Hughes

Ben Johnson

Tchaik Chassey and James Gowan

much boosted by the fact that Nick had won the prize for the Berlin Stock Exchange only three days before. Finally there was Richard Rogers with something which was a bit unusual, a model made out of Meccano which we could all fiddle and play with.

I can't say how our pavilion related to the other pavilions, because in the time available one couldn't really (and perhaps this was a positive asset of the Biennale) co-ordinate everything to too tight a programme. One thing we did stress throughout was the buildability of all the project drawings. The models and photographs related to buildings which had been or could be put up, even John Outram's Utopian designs were related to quite real or realisable projects. I think this is what gave a particular kind of flavour. Beyond that, we were coming to it fairly fresh and there was a degree of apprehension on the side of the architectural profession, as we had no experience in organising architectural exhibitions. But it was a very happy working relationship and I think we both learned a great deal from one another. What does concern me for the future is the fact that it is very difficult to get political and financial backing in this country compared to countries like France, who seem to find it much easier. For instance, the French minister visited accompanied by something like 30 politicians and local mayors, which was a very formidable turnout.

Ben Johnson: I've spent much time looking at the world of architecture, yet I'm an outsider to the world of architecture so I haven't had to align myself with any current movements. My personal view of the exhibition as a whole was how very diverse it was. I've just been the objective observer, fascinated by the quality of individual architects as well as the architecture reflecting personality and people within that society. What I was seeing in this show was the fact that we live in a very large world where almost anything can happen. We had here in this show the great diversity of the Japanese, Hungarian, Polish, Russian and British. If we look at the British Pavilion it summed up a very good pavilion wherein people were given a great deal of freedom to represent themselves. I found the French pavilion very disappointing and very disturbing because I think it was an exercise in graphic design and therefore a product of a graphic designer and not a group of architects, but I know that some people thought it was a very important and powerful way of presenting architecture.

One of the pavilions I enjoyed very much was Tessenow. I found it a curious choice with very disturbing images and it made me wonder whether we are looking back to go forward; whether we think that perhaps the enthusiasm for Post-Modernism may well have been a promotion of fashion journals. Perhaps we need to assess things a little more carefully towards the end of the 20th century. I was also very interested in the Russian pavilion and the way that one went from Constructivist and Suprematist imagery to Deconstructionist and it wasn't difficult to take that jump of 50, 60, or more years.

The whole atmosphere of Italy is very special, Venice in itself is special, but it is also a country which appreciates culture and is not afraid of the academic or the cultured person. In this country we have a fear of cultural professionalism and I think that the Biennale wouldn't have worked here, quite apart from the fact that we don't have an appropriate venue. I would like to believe that it's just the very beginning of the breakdown of barriers between artist, engineer, architect, and scientist. We started to get hints of it in this show, there were several architects making sculptures and paintings to represent their work with artists involved in the presentation, and also there was a great deal of input from engineers which sadly lacked recognition. I believe we're entering a bigger world, a world where we may start to learn from each other.

Paul Finch: I'd like to ask Jim Stirling to say something about his building which was the star of the show. I wonder if you might say where you saw your building in the context of the Biennale and the context of that location as a whole, and perhaps whether you think that the concept of an architecture of Pluralism has validity.

James Stirling: Well, to deal with the last point first, I hate labelling, all of these phrases like Post-Modern, High-Tech and Neo-Classical are cheap journalism. I think there's only good architecture, boring architecture and bad architecture. I mean, the very fact that it's got this title, the 'Architecture of Pluralism', is enough to turn me off coming here. I think all this labelling is really a cheap, sloppy and lazy way for journalists to write about architecture and I think it gives everybody a bad name.

James Stirling

With regard to the Biennale, the thing that I particularly liked about it was the conjunction of the Corderie, which is this huge, long building going into infinity in relationship to the garden. I suppose the square footage of space in the Corderie is approximate to that of the combined pavilions in the garden, but the difference is that the Corderie is a single immensely long building into the bays of which students and everybody else make their exhibitions. The garden contains these pavilions which are small, so you get the juxtaposition of the urban experience of the Corderie and a kind of garden experience of the pavilions. I think these two places are within walking distance of each other in Venice and it's the combination of these two places which was so interesting, to oscillate from one to the other.

There is not really very much to say about the bookshop. It is a very small and modest building, but it is a building which I greatly enjoyed being involved with. It could not have happened without Francesco Dal Co, he was our client. In fact, he was much more than a client because amongst other things he was responsible for getting through the 37 separate *permissos* politically necessary for this small building.

The first building was built in the Biennale Gardens in 1895 and the last, 15 years ago. Our site is close to a theatre garden in the trees, lining up with one of the main footpaths into the garden. Whether you come from the lagoon or from Venice you arrive very close to where the bookshop is sited. We originally started by trying to make a building which was symmetrical on a corner, an octagonal or circular building which could focus on either of the avenues there. We thought there was no possibility of removing any trees, not a single tree, from the gardens so we couldn't find the ground for it. We ended up by sliding the bookshop into the avenue of trees.

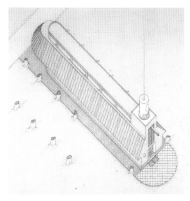

James Stirling and Michael Wilford, Bookshop, axonometric

You enter the bookshop from a circular terrace into a single room which has a glass window that goes all the way around both sides and is probably the longest single shop window in the whole of Venice. It has 50 metres of display-top for the books and a counter for checking in and checking out as well as a small storeroom with a safe and a lavatory. There is a boardwalk which goes all the way around the building where the public walk, look in on to the bookshelf, see the books, and if they are interested in something they will then come in to browse and perhaps purchase. The end of the boardwalk finishes with a square edge, whereas the end of the building finishes with a circular edge. This creates a covered space where people can listen to music events in the theatre garden or to speeches, or friends can just hang around and meet. There is now a flight of steps at the level change between the boardwalk and the footpath. None of the existing trees were taken away, they cut into the boardwalk and in fact almost touch the over-hanging eaves of the roof. In other words, it was the distance between the trees which conditioned the span of the roof design. The trees take on the aspect of columns along the closure of the overhang which is something I didn't anticipate, but I really like the almost architectural relationship of the trees to the building. Before, I thought of them as being a nuisance because the radius and the dimensions of the building were entirely conditioned by the trees. In the end the trees were a real architectural plus, though we had to go through an elaborate treatment of them which would allow water to get to the roots.

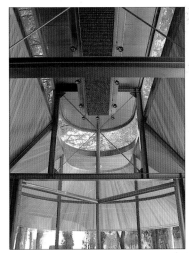

James Stirling and Michael Wilford, Bookshop, view of ceiling and roof structure

An axonometric view of the entrance terrace shows the boardwalk all the way around, the entrance door and a ventilation grille above with plant space on top of it over which there's a big illuminated lantern with the Electa bookshop signs. Out of the very top of the bookshop comes a laser which goes up and is visible from the Lagoon. It's had some faults but in future it will be a perfectly straight line going up announcing the Biennale events into the night. The idea of the copper roof is to provide shade and cover for people going around the boardwalk and viewing the books through the shop window. The ceiling is in redwood, which extends out of the building to create an overhang

Martin Spring and Geoffrey Broadbent

Peter Ahrends

that provides public space at the end of the building. The roof has ridges so that ventilation occurs on the under edge. The perforated copper allows ventilation up inside it and overflows from the roof go down through it, any water just spills onto the copper. Eventually the copper will stain the boardwalk below and it also will go green.

With regard to the British pavilion, the first I got to know about it was a phone call saying, 'we have a problem, we've got to fill the British pavilion and we don't know what to do and we've no money. How about putting your exhibition from Bologna into the entire pavilion?' And I said, 'well, the Italians have seen the exhibition in Bologna and I don't want to repeat myself'. A few days later he called back and said 'well, now we have a group of six architects and you're in the middle room and how will you think about it from there?' So then I thought about the middle room and four other rooms around it, and I realised everybody would circulate through the middle room most of the time, so nothing big could be in the middle room on the floor, no big models. I assumed that the others would focus on the huge blow-up photograph and the big model so then I thought I would have nothing in the middle of the floor and a lot of tiny things on the walls so there would be a rare juxtaposition between the centre room and the flanking rooms. I didn't phone up Richard or Norman or anybody and ask them what they were doing, I just made the assumption that the others would mainly have big models and huge photographs. I'm glad that I opted for tiny postage stamps stuck on the wall and nothing in the middle of the floor.

Geoffrey Broadbent: I interviewed Andreas Papadakis and we talked at length about Pluralism, although I spoke to him this morning and he said he didn't believe in it anymore. About 20 years ago, he inherited a magazine called *Architectural Design*. It was fairly broad-minded even at that time; it got the first rumblings of green architecture and Cybernetic smatterings and he carried on with that tradition of publishing everything that came in, not editing out things he didn't like. And he said, 'that made a lot of friends for me and even more enemies,' because there were people who thought there's one true faith of Modernism in architecture and anything else was therefore wrong, immoral and should be stopped immediately. Fairly early on in the days of *AD*, he published an issue on Post-Modernism, a little book by Charles Jencks; he gave Zaha Hadid the prestigious *AD* Gold Medal Award and published Bernard Tschumi's *Manhattan Transcripts*. Any one of those could have caught on in the early 70s, but the one the public bought was called Post-Modernism. He said, 'I wasn't responsible for that, I didn't invent it. The public insisted that we printed more about that.' And I believe he's right. There are these currents that go on that you don't control, that I don't control, that Jim doesn't control, but they are movements of various kinds.

I do think we need labels, because we have to cope with things. In the British pavilion there are four architects we all would call High-tech, and there are two that we would call Suprematist. It's useful to be able to cope with the world, to have that kind of clarity of distinction between different ways of doing things. Pluralism really comes from a much broader field than architecture, it's in politics too. Somewhat like that hand game where you make a stone, paper, or scissors and scissors cut paper, paper wraps stone etc, the political systems you're dealing with are exactly that kind; stone is the hard heart of capitalism, paper is the bureaucracy of socialism and anarchy is the scissors cutting through. Without those three going on simultaneously, things wouldn't move and progress. It's exactly the same in architecture now, we need these various currents interacting with each other, attacking each other, in order to progress. It's not a question of anything goes, but of distinguishing the good, the boring and the bad within each of these categories. If we didn't have them our lives would be very much impoverished with just one thing going on.

Peter Ahrends: I don't know what Geoffrey Broadbent actually means by a movement. I don't actually see in what way Pluralism can be defined as a movement. If you, within living memory, cast your mind back to Frank Lloyd Wright, Lubetkin, Voysey, Mackintosh, the Russian Constructivists, Corbusier, then one must conclude that there's nothing new because it's always existed. The fact that there are different strands of interest and different preoccupations being presented at any one moment to society, is evident and it's evidently not new. I want to have defined, by those who have a mind to do so, what Pluralism as a movement is intended to consist of. If you're putting forward a case for Pluralism as an entity it must therefore have some boundaries which can be usefully defined – either from a theoretical stand-point or from a very straight, 'man-in-the-street' position – what it is about as a kind of inspection of a cultural pursuit.

John Melvin

John Melvin: I was wondering if I might answer that by asking a question. Pluralism is meant to be this new freedom and you see a demand for political freedom taking place weekly. During the course of the Biennale, a large part of Europe was in turmoil and peoples who had hitherto been constrained by blocs and ideologies were demanding that their freedom, their history, their nationhood, and their individuality be recognised after 50 years of repression. I think the Modern movement in its early avant-garde days associated itself with certain scientific objects which led to that repression. I'm not saying this was intentional, but there was an ideology that was sympathetic to this. This has now broken down, people who have been repressed have seen this as totalitarianism. It's brought chaos and ruin to their countries, it hasn't delivered the goods. How does this affect architecture? Does architecture have any connection with our moral life? The early pioneers of Modernism thought it did. Do we now still maintain this connection, and if there is a connection, are we able to express this demand for history, can we reflect nationhood, can we reflect the desire for a face? These are the intangible things which people are demanding, it's a real demand. If this Pluralism is painting with a broader palette, are we still painting in numbers? Are we actually saying something new in Pluralism or is it just a different means to say the same old thing?

Martin Pawley

Martin Pawley: I'd like to respond to that and make the only point that very forcibly struck me at the Biennale. It's tempting to say that Pluralism is internationalising; I think that would be a very succinct answer to Mr Melvin's question in that it's able to deal with the kinds of disruption of history affected by the 20th century which can be amazingly seen in the pavilions themselves. I think you have to distinguish, if you're going to follow this line of thought, between architects, architecture and architectural exhibitions. I think architects are already international, they are more international than their exhibitions. At the exhibition we heard that Nick Grimshaw was going to design the Stock Exchange in Berlin, and Jeremy Dixon and Ed Jones were going to build a bus station in Venice. This is how architects live, of course you have to be successful to live that way, but that's a completely international style of existence that wasn't reflected in the exhibitions.

I think you've got a situation where you have to face the fact that architecture is already Pluralistic. Architects are international and the most obsolete element in the whole thing are architectural exhibitions which are somehow locked in an old national pride mode. They actually haven't kept up with the practice of architecture, we can see the obsolescence of real architecture in those pavilions at the Biennale, all of which were hidden by trees because they've got so many skeletons in their cupboard that you don't open them up.

Lebbeus Woods: What is this Pluralism about? Is it simply a matter of interchangeable styles that are somehow products architects are placing in a kind of global market place from where people can buy as they choose, or perhaps, is it an architecture connected with the vital life of a culture or people? I think this is a very fundamental issue, I'm glad you raised it because I think this word Pluralism suggests almost a department store of products or of styles rather than of real substance or real ideas related to human life. I think that's a topic we can certainly discuss. With the issue of eastern and central Europe for example, what role can architecture play in their emergence out of this period other than as an emblem of emerging from the Communist regime into consumerist society? Do they hire the famous architects of the West to design their buildings to prove that now they're as good as the West or entering

Lebbeus Woods

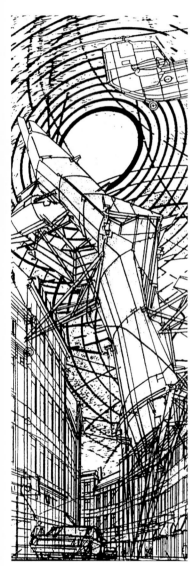

*Lebbeus Woods, Zagreb-Free-Zone,
Freespace structure, detail*

the same sphere of culture as the West, or does architecture have the possibility of participating in some kind of cultural regeneration of these countries? Those seem to be the really vital issues to me and if this Pluralism has any content, that is the only area that I would be interested in discussing.

It wasn't until very recently that I finally gathered the courage, or in a way had the occasion to address some actual urban situations both in Berlin and Zagreb. Architecture and the city are as indivisible conceptually and even tectonically as the individual is from society. I think it's absolutely essential to consider both at the same time.

I am much more interested in the secret life of the city, those things which can maybe happen out of sight or in a kind of unseen way, strange things, things that are unexplainable, even unjustifiable in terms of any sort of convention of society or certainly of architecture. I decided to bring to the city some kinds of spaces that didn't exist already. Not knowing what to do has never stopped me, so I just simply began by introducing some strange configurations, some kind of foreign presence entering the city. I saw these as structures, a kind of tectonic manifestation, a kind of form that was not quite yet architecture, not something inhabitable in fact, inhabiting a kind of abstract zone. I began to call these freespace structures. I know that free is a very difficult word to use, but I meant it in this sense; free of any kind of predetermined meaning or usefulness. Really they are meaningless and useless spaces so that there's no way that we know from our former experience what these might be used for.

In the city of Zagreb I proposed a free-zone project that was an extension of the Berlin project, but with some different ideas. There, it takes on a different meaning in terms of the political conditions, a country emerging from Socialism. In Zagreb, there's a big difference in that the freespace structures are not hidden in the buildings, but are actively in the streets. The idea was to let them be a presence in the streets without completely disrupting the streets, so they have to stand on a very small point. Structurally they either lean against strong, lateral conditions on existing buildings such as a party wall condition or an end-wall condition, or are in some way suspended between those same strong points. Inside is a capsule of instrumentation that links this small structure with other points in the city and in the world. The very important aspect of these projects is the fact that they really *are* mobile, they are not self-propelled but they can be moved. This is an idea that offends a lot of architects who feel that architecture can only happen in relation to a given site or a given context, but the mobility of these is important because they have to stay fluid themselves. Architecture as an instrument of transformation embraces with equal intensity of feeling and thought all conditions of physicality. It has no taste for the metaphysical, but is relentlessly materialistic. The visible and the invisible are terms referring to bands on the electromagnetic spectrum. Thus the self-referentiality of transformation is established, the recursive loop between invention and perception given its mechanics. The comforts of tautology and solipsism are voided by dialogue: individual existence is confirmed only by and in an *other*. By establishing boundaries, an architecture of transformation demands their violation.

Richard McCormac: To try to thread some of the contributions together, one should consider the breakdown of so-called Modernism. One aspect of its dissolution is the recognition that European cities have a structure that needs to be reconstituted rather than taken to pieces. That could be seen as part of the Plurality of architecture but on the other hand it actually makes quite a different kind of demand which was the sense that the questions about civic value and society's values are more embedded in ideas about cities than they are in any other part of our visual culture. So it seems to me that one of the fundamental questions about architecture is to what extent architecture is under obligation to the conventions and proprieties of cities and to what extent it should be allowed to be quite free of those obligations and much more conceptual and anarchic.

Rob Krier: Your speeches are so complicated I can't understand them, that's my bad English! I was confused by what I saw in Venice. I am completely depressed by the number of things which have nothing to do with the art of building and the art of construction. Imagine the style, the discipline the 20s had; coming from a classical education they knew how to put things together and they had a very good attitude on how to organise a building and how to construct in an extremely intelligent way, and what is going on now? In the 20s we were conscious of a compositional discipline and a repertoire of architectural elements. I couldn't give any comment on Deconstructive matters because Coop Himmelblau are my friends in Vienna and I have respect for them, but nobody could imagine 20 years ago that they could be successful – putting chimneys in all directions and making urban design layouts just like Meccano games, which makes absolutely no sense at all.

Peter Cook

Peter Cook: This whole question of the -isms is a question of labelling for public consumption. It has so little to do with the fire that's in the belly when I hear any real architect talk. Basically it describes things not by the way that they're done but through the literary distortion or pictorial distortion, and I think that the fire in the belly comes from what I can only call an architectural direction which is a whole series of things. But then I would fall into the trap of labelling, but architectural things are sometimes triggered by grappling with some organisational issue. They don't stay like that, but they might be triggered by figurative issues or something that suddenly gets you moving. Or they might be triggered by operational issues, making people bother about whether they're outside the building or not, or where they come in the door or how they get out. Or they might be manipulative, by which I don't mean those issues so much as the sort of thing that you do on the drawing board and you say 'this will amuse them', meaning the two or three people that you like to amuse. And also they are to do with materiality or any mixture of these, some operational thing that suddenly has a figurative trigger or a materiality issue which suddenly suggests that something might be porous or damp and therefore, however you draw it you can't really explain it.

Giles Worsley

Literary and pictorial terms are poor things. The best English language critics still alive, Colin Rowe and Ken Frampton, not only had an architectural training but have actually built things. They have been through a series of passing inspirations and I think that therefore, the whole issue is to do with a much more subtle dropping of markers between architects. Two or more architects may meet together from moment to moment and share a couple of enthusiasms and for that moment, they are on the same side of an unspoken firing line, they are allies. I think this question of shared enthusiasm from 'triggers' is extremely difficult even to the inside outsider because it's to do with partly gut instinct, wit and testing. This is why those of us who spend most of our time as academics, if we're not good at it, fall into the same traps as the journalists; we label, we compartment, we tell students that they should follow a certain procedure of connecting these labels and they'll be able to turn it on like a TV set.

I think that if this daft Pluralism thing happened to cause two or three people who wouldn't otherwise have been in the same town or the same room or the same bar at the same time, to be there, then I have the suspicion, speaking as Cedric Price would say, 'from a position of unassailable ignorance', it is a step in the right direction. I suspect that in earlier years, the Biennale would have been organised so that such a variety of people probably wouldn't have been in the same place at the same time. But in the end I think it's the nerve endings that are important. If it just gets a few more people talking to each other and perhaps meeting by accident, then it has a value, but if it is to support some critic's dream, it has no value at all.

Piers Gough

Piers Gough: Peter Davey said to me that he's never seen a building in his magazine that was symmetrical. And so I don't know whether your bookshop will get in Jim, but yes, the architectural establishment certainly likes to divide people up and to characterise those big particular kinds of architects, there's no doubt about that and Pluralism is very attractive. It's horribly attractive, in fact this thing's really screwing me up because the older I get the more things I think I could do and so I envy people who are single-minded and think it's all about one thing. I don't know where they get it from or actually how they retain it because when you've seen Coop Himmelblau put together a building, all that talk about having to have a classical basis doesn't seem to be very important anymore, does it?

Ian Ritchie

Ian Ritchie: I was struck by the popularisation of Pluralism. I remember coming from Giscard d'Estaing when he was President of France and he put forward the competition for La Villette, the museum. In the letter to the architect he actually asked that you didn't come into this building in sneakers. When the Socialists came in a couple of years later, they rewrote the brief and they spent the whole weekend discussing this very issue of how the potential clients actually create a situation for the social statement that architects can then interpret, can actually swing from one to the other. I thought that was actually quite Pluralistic in that there's a freedom for one political party or the other to change.

Dimitri Fatouros: Let's keep the label Pluralism. I would like to play with the words and say for instance, neutral is Pluralism, but I'm not going near this dangerous word-play. Maybe we have to see Pluralism not in the works of the masters and leaders but in the work of their followers. In real life, a construct is a realisation of their follower's work and not of the main leaders. This is one point.

Dimitri Fatouros

The second point is that it seems to me that despite a lot of discussion of Pluralism, there are at least two common underlying features. One is that we'll have gigantism all around the world as well as an acceptance and obedience to technology. This happens in any kind of plural situation. The style does not prevent the acceptance and the obedience to gigantism and this is a fact very well known in France. This marriage of technology with gigantism produces all the major events of today's well-known Pluralism. It seems to me, and we may see this in Dal Co's Biennale, that there is an absence of interest in nature. I would say that it is only Stirling's bookshop that has a dialogue with nature. To my mind the majority of the works presented, of the works discussed, are quite apart from a continuous dialogue with nature. Nature has a love affair with architecture.

I have a very practical point to make, finally. This presentation of the Biennale is certainly the biggest event of architecture ever and I consider this as a very important fact for contemporary culture. For good or bad doesn't count, the fact is that it is extremely important for human culture. Despite this, we see most of the cinema discussed for weeks and weeks in newspapers and mass media. This doesn't happen with architecture. This means something, either the mass media does not consider architecture as a creative endeavour and they see it as a politician's affair or a business affair, or they don't think our work produces the *stimuli* which will develop the sensitivity and the concern of the public.

Robert Adam

Robert Adam: One of the problems is the use of the word Pluralism, I don't know of any architect sitting around here who's going to turn around and say 'I am a Pluralist, therefore I do a Pluralist building'. Pluralism rather suggests that we are in a 'situation of Plurality', which is really a return to normal. For a relatively brief period of time, we had a state of affairs where you couldn't admit that any sort of Plurality was tolerable. What we have now is a situation where people will admit some sort of Plurality of views. It's a tolerable situation to exist. What I find interesting about it is that if we're talking about Pluralism, we're also talking about the break up of Modernism as a sole view. A Yugoslav friend of mine said 'old Modernists are like old communists, they don't understand the revolution's over'.

What interests me is that there are lots of people who might on the surface claim some adherence to Pluralism but deep down they say 'well, I'm only building good buildings or bad buildings'. The trouble with good and bad is that very often the word 'bad' is used to exclude certain aspects of things that might otherwise be considered to be Plural.

Martin Pawley: It's not whether any architect would stand up and say 'I am a Pluralist', it's whether any architect would stand up and say 'I am not a Pluralist'. Now, I don't think you'd be very likely to get anyone to do that. I think really it's a kind of Esperanto, it's a language with all kinds of accommodations like one of those little pocket devices that translate several hundred words from different languages into different languages. Of course it gets some of the words wrong, it loses some of the nuances, but basically we all understand it, we all use the same machine and that's what Pluralism has become now.

Richard McCormac: In my experience of building buildings, in a practice which has been going for nearly two decades, there is an experience of actually reacting to situations which are so different to each other, culturally speaking and in the kinds of requirements that are being made of us, that I can't imagine it being anything other than under some sort of label which is very complicated. In fact we try to avoid being describable in any simple way. But if you think of current schemes either being built or on the drawing board – a training building for a science-based international company, an underground station, a large building for an Oxford College, an old people's community home – all those things to me require responses to the clients and to the circumstances which are incredibly different to each other. I can't imagine a lot of architects actually being able to do it because a lot of us get into situations where

Richard McCormac

we are able to do what it is we want to do, and we actually avoid the situations where we can't if we have a certain ideological line to push forward. Those of us who work in England and try to get planning permission and work for very different sorts of clients can hardly be in that very simple frame of mind which Piers Gough was admiring, and which I greatly admire in certain architects. I couldn't conceive of getting work done for many clients if I had such a frame of mind. Is that Pluralism?

Hugh Pearman: I think there is an uneasiness in this room because everybody knows that James Stirling was entirely right from the very start because there are actual architects, real architects in this room, who should have nothing to do with this extraordinary process of discussing this work. It's a question of semantics and it's only for the critics to decide. Maybe the architects should withdraw, maybe they should have left the moment James said that, because it's entirely true. Then the rest of us who don't build buildings can sit around and decide what we're going to call it this week. It is, of course, a ridiculous attempt to sell magazines and that's the way all magazines and all journalists function.

Hugh Pearman

Lebbeus Woods: I find myself in the unusual position of somehow defending journalism in architecture but for God's sake, what's wrong with it? I mean, if one is a journalist, one writes about architecture as part of the world that we inhabit. What are they to contribute? Are they merely to go to James and say, 'what shall I say this week James, should I mention Pluralism or not?' Hell no, these people are trying to sort out a complex landscape and see what kind of geography there is and no, we're not going to like it. I don't think architects are going to go around embracing this stuff, but why can't we admit it into the culture of architecture? We can debate it, which I think is the purpose of this, but why do we have to get up and leave the room? What kind of people are we? Are we so small- or narrow-minded that we have to walk out when someone mentions an idea?

Richard McCormac: The Traditionalist argument, epitomised by somebody like Marcus Binney, is still over-simplification, it's grotesque it's so redundant. Nevertheless, I think there is a real need for a publicly accessible architectural criticism and the terminology of that criticism. I don't know what the words ought to be and I think it's quite right to try to debate that here today.

View of the Pop Art Exhibition with Ian Pollard

James Stirling: I think it's the huge quantity of terminologies which are the problem. I think there's an excess of labels and terms. I remember Ada Louise Huxtable who, when she went to make a review of a building for *The New York Times*, hardly used any of these words. She went to the building and she went through it and she wrote about her

Paul Koralek

Peter Cook

Botond Bognar

experience of visiting the building and didn't refer to these kinds of terms at all, so you usually got an original and sincere appreciation of a piece of architecture and I, for that reason, always liked reading her work. If anybody were to ask me if I was a Pluralist or if I was not a Pluralist, I would be embarrassed either way. I would prefer to say, I hope I'm an architect.

Paul Koralek: I think we would all agree that variety is a good thing, we would all agree that tolerance is a good thing. The problem comes with the criteria which we use to say whether it's a good building or not and I think I would say in the end, whatever theories and arguments I used to try and define that, finally it's my gut feeling as to what I think is good or not that counts. There are criteria and I suspect we disagree very strongly about those criteria that go into what is a good building. I'm sure that within this room there would be some very strong disagreements about those criteria and that is where I begin to have the courage to wonder whether I am a Pluralist, because certainly I believe in my own criteria and I suspect that each architect here believes in his own criteria. To find out to what extent those criteria overlap and coincide with each other and to find out where and why they differ would be quite difficult but very interesting.

Kirstin Feireiss: My experience is that architectural writers have problems if they do not have a word and a style in their hands. They need 'Constructivism' and 'Deconstructivism', they can't live without words like this. It's a big problem because these styles don't exist for the architects and normally, in previous centuries, the name for the style was coined 40 years later. I hate the word Pluralism because it's nothing and everything and I can't work with it. Modern-Pluralism I can't understand because Pluralism was there all the time.

I was at the Biennale and for me it was extremely interesting because it not only showed the architecture of the country but also the ways government worked. Normally most countries don't like to make experiments, I feel they count on the heroes. I liked the pavilion from the USA because it was put together very intelligently. The British Pavilion was however a little bit too mixed, the German situation was terrible and very much discussed because although the Tessenow exhibition was liked, he's a dead architect and the concept of the Biennale is to show new architects. I think it demonstrates the way that the German government has absolutely no idea of architecture as a cultural aspect. I liked the Hungarian pavilion which showed a very simple, clear and honest way way of working in architecture.

Botond Bognar: I have never felt that the Japanese entertained this kind of idea of Pluralism but obviously there is a broad spectrum of intentions going on. Pluralism is a good phrase for the market place as far as stylistics are concerned, as we tend to approach architecture on the surface. Maybe there are some inherent values to architecture which are specific to architecture. On the other hand, there are values which are added to it and are specific to certain political, economic, cultural, geographical conditions in which architecture is caught up in and cannot escape. The question today is what kind of culture are we talking about in the global market place, what is the value of a national culture, and how do we define that? This brings me back to the Japanese culture and I'm confronted with the question, what is Japanese about Japanese architecture? The Japanese have been caught up in an information society even before we knew the term. Their culture has been shaped all through history by the introduction, stealing or borrowing of other cultures. It started with the Korean, the Chinese and then of course, eventually the Western culture and they find themselves part and parcel of this flux of information. So what is Japanese architecture in this information society? They build according to the type of technology that they have.

Peter Cook: I will declare my hand: my credentials for being here are as a liberal, mechanistic romantic. I find that the

Japanese have by-passed most of the hocus-pocus that has been talked about. They are of course child-like, or perhaps what they have retained the issue of delight in architecture. This delight is intertwined with an incredible system of recognitions and placements and sensitivities and yet also naughty, nasty and funny things. Of course the British favourite among the Japanese architects is probably Tadao Ando, because he has taste in the European, correct sense. I think he's a good architect, but he's not an interesting architect to my mind as a child – correction – as a liberal, mechanistic romantic.

Ernst Schneider

Paul Finch: If there is an architectural Pluralism, it is happening at the time when political Pluralism is of course coming to an end, and it's not inconceivable there will be nothing but liberal democracies within the very near future. I wonder what implications that might have for architecture on both sides of what used to be the Iron Curtain, and perhaps in a sort of flashy, superficial, journalistic way, I might throw out a definition of Pluralism that's just come into my head, which is the architecture of Peaceful Coexistence.

Let's pick up the point that has been made by many of the architects here about the usefulness of critical definitions and the whole attempt to put things into pigeon holes and come up with critical approaches to what it is that people do and why they do it, and to put it into some sort of historical and social context.

Martin Pawley: I was moved by Richard McCormac's statement that 'we try not to be describable in any way,' which I think expresses the critic's predicament, because the critic has no career unless he or she can describe something in some way. All architects, all the ones that I've ever met over 20 years or so, always try to fight labels. They always want to be treated as individual cases, where the world consists of millions and millions of utterly specific events and is immune to all generalisation. If we apply that to architecture we then get 26,000 special cases in this country and perhaps 120,000 special cases in Italy, and so on. How a critic could manage to deal on a weekly or monthly basis with this vast universe of architects certainly would defeat me. A universe like this truly would be indescribable. It would be like having no plural for the word man or woman, just as in one Eskimo language where you simply say man, man, man, man, man for as many men as there are present. Or, a better illustration is of course Crocodile Dundee's attempt to say hello to everyone in New York as he walks down the street. Clearly critics can't work if you accept that architects can't be defined except as individual artists who should all be treated understandingly as separate cases, because the understanding of the reader or the viewer becomes impossible if architecture is treated in that way. If there are no generalisations possible about architecture, then architecture itself becomes an indescribable thing, no longer a unitary phenomenon.

View of the Pop Art Exhibition

James Stirling: You would treat a novelist as himself, you would treat a painter as himself.

Martin Pawley: But novelists are grouped into schools and treated in the same way as architects. You may deplore the purpose.

View of the Pop Art Exhibition with Piers Gough

James Stirling: If you are writing about a particular novelist or painter, you would write about him. I think most writers do write about the specific person.

Andreas Papadakis: You are today in a gallery where there is an exhibition called 'Pop Art', which is yet another abbreviation to explain a group of artists.

James Stirling: There are many references to the architect or architects in a gross collective way, which seems not to

Kenneth Powell

Sara Gordon

View of the Pop Art Exhibition

address them as individuals. Perhaps I've got it wrong.

Martin Pawley: I was merely underlining the impossibility of treating each architect as a specific case. But these cheap generalisations, terms like Modernism, Post-Modernism, High-Tech, Classical, Gothic, all these are of course short-hand terms.

They are useful in discourse because they convey possibly erroneous, but as I would now argue, powerful meanings. They're powerful because they are believed to be understood by a large number of people who then, when confronted with a printed page or some other medium, see some item or an event which they can understand and follow. It is not like a sign that says 'the next two columns are written in Greek', it is like a sign that uses some words you are familiar with, so that you then proceed to read it. Now this is the sort of media-as-an-industry view of why terms like that should be used. When I'm confronted by an architect who doesn't want to be defined by a cheap label, I wonder how he would prefer to be treated. In fact, architects really benefit from this. Now as to the power of this type of definition, I could take the arch categoriser, Charles Jencks himself: his book on Post-Modernism has gone through six editions and sold more than 140,000 copies. The impact of that book will last longer than most buildings, and its influence can be illustrated by a point he made to me; he showed me 15 critical references to Sir Richard Rogers as a Post-Modern architect, written by social critics admired one way or another in their field. Charles Jencks' question, which I think is a very good one, is 'Does this raise the point that we should say, is Richard Rogers a Post-Modernist, or does it raise the even more ominous question that it doesn't matter what Sir Richard Rogers thinks, he is, in history, going to be classed as a Post-Modernist.' Architects are aware that critics in the end will decide whether Richard Rogers is a Post-Modernist, whether Sir Norman Foster is a Modernist and whether all the architects here are Pluralists or not. It will not be decided by architects, it will be decided by critics. And I think, finally, that all the architects here would prefer that situation to one in which they were treated as special cases and the buildings were treated as special cases, where the work of the structural engineer, the service engineers, the component suppliers, the contract managers, the clients and the finances were discussed at equal length to that of the architect. If that happened, we would reach a point where architecture would cease to be a unitary phenomenon that could be written about, spoken about, or televised for anyone at all.

Kevin Rowbotham: I've had a number of difficulties listening to what's been said. I guess the first thing I wondered about was why everybody seems to be talking about the same kind of Pluralism, which seemed to me to be very anti-Pluralistic. It seemed to me that we're discussing the Pluralism of form and not the Pluralism of content and I wonder how architects might react to different political contexts with respect to the form of their building, as if a Pluralism of content might set the agenda rather than the Pluralism of form. I think that with respect to the notion of social context, what we engage in is a very private conversation which is aimed at a very specific socio-metric group. I wonder whether it would be possible to make a kind of popular architectural language which came from critics and architects, which everybody could understand because it seems to me that architecture of itself is a particular kind of thing which has as its nature something exclusive. It talks in a particular, very detailed way about a part of the world.

What kind of popular language would it be? If we might reconstruct architecture from the beginning, if we had no architects at all, we might ask people to become experts in that area, and they would then develop a series of ways of reading the world which were very specialised. I find it paradoxical that architects lament the misinterpretation of critics because it seems to me that magazine and TV culture are certainly much more powerful than architecture itself. There may be a lot of people visiting the Pompidou Centre for instance, but the general architectural culture – even of students – is produced by critics, magazines and television, and these are, at the centre of a kind of architectural understanding, infinitely more powerful than the buildings themselves. In the age of information, the people who are controlling the cultural ideas aren't architects at all, architects have ceased to be important. The only attachment we have to architects is fostered by a notion of sentimentality. If we were really to look at the issue before us, we would look at how the dissemination of architectural culture takes place because that is the source of what might be called Pluralism.

Geoffrey Broadbent: On the question of education, I am an unabashed Pluralist. When I first arrived in Portsmouth in 1967, I said I have a model for this school of architecture, it's Mies van der Rohe at IIT. My school will be exactly the opposite of that. In Mies' case, you have to design it his way, with steel and glass. I want a course where students are encouraged to do their own things and then we challenge them as to whether what they do is good. We've been a Pluralist school, because literally in the same studio we have Classical and Deconstruction design going on. In the Biennale something like 17 schools world-wide had that kind of range, and that seems to me to be true Pluralism.

Tomàs Taveira and Suha Özkar

Tomás Taveira: It seems to me that in fact this word Pluralism is more a moral and political word. An architect is an individual and we need to be treated as such. But we cannot avoid the classifications. When I studied in the Lisbon School of Architecture, everybody had to be narrow, nobody could use their imagination. Today, what happens is rather similar. Due to the power of the School of Architecture in Porto, the media, the government officials, and the Portuguese Architectural Association, everybody does the same project if they want to get the first prize in a competition. Everybody has to do something minimal, puritan and simple if they want to be recognised by the critics or the media. I am living in a country where the word Pluralist doesn't apply to politics. I would say that the work of the critics and the media has had a good effect in spreading new ideas.

Pluralism must be included in the schools just to avoid this kind of misunderstanding or misusing of democracy. But using certain kinds of definitions in a political and moral way is provoking a great deal of prejudice in my country.

Lebbeus Woods: Why can't we just accept what the press does? It's going to do what it wants to do anyway and of course we're not going to like it, but thank God it is free and out of our control. If architects controlled the press, they would produce exactly the same sort of situation you see in Portugal. I want to move to something else that I think is a lot more important. I'm wondering why whenever there's a gathering of architects like this, they're afraid to discuss this political or social aspect of architecture. I think there's a feeling perhaps, and I can speak from my own negative instincts about this, that somehow it's against architecture to speak about society or about the politics that architecture arises from and which it in fact serves. I don't think this is the case at all, I think all architecture is political by definition. From the word go, whether we want to discuss it or admit it or carry on a conversation about it, it's still political. For example, I see the work of James Stirling – not discussing it from an architectural critique, but from a social critique or a political critique – as one which serves extremely well the existing structure of authority in our society and that's why you're able to get buildings built. The practice of architecture today is protected from confrontation with changing political conditions in the world within a hermetically sealed capsule of professionalism, which ostensibly exists to protect its high standards from the corrupting influence of political expediency and merely topical concerns. Architects themselves are complicit with this lie to the extent that they know it is enforced by the very institutions and individuals who commission the buildings they design, and who have a profound economic and social interest in maintaining a *status quo* in which they hold the highest authority. Professionalism separates architects from people and their need to change the conditions of their existence, which is the essence of all politics. Far from protecting the high standards of architecture, this separation impoverishes architectural work, reducing its productions to tokens of power, at best, and – at worst – to instruments of destruction.

Tomàs Taveira, New Building Project, Lisbon, drawing

There are other architects, Peter Cook, Zaha Hadid, Coop Himmelblau, who are struggling just to keep the few jobs

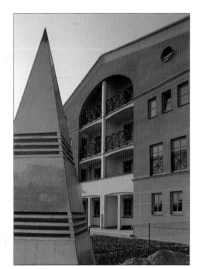

Rob Krier, House Feilner,
Schinkelplatz, Berlin

Rob Krier, Gateway, Rauchstrasse,
Berlin

they have. They are celebrated architects, we all admire their work, but they can't get projects built. Why? Because in their work there are political ideas, ideas that challenge the existing structure of authority and therefore, they're not going to get the commissions, they're going to have to fight for them. This political dimension of architecture I think is a much more fruitful domain for discussion as to what is conveyed in terms of political or social meaning by the various ways of working in architecture.

One final comment on that. We live in a world that is incredibly involved with these issues. The newspapers don't write about architecture or whether a certain building, a certain style, or a certain word is the burning issue of the day; the newspapers are filled with political events, social events on all scales. It seems to me that architects are deathly afraid to address the relation of their work to these issues that affect the rest of society.

Andreas Papadakis: I don't think it's a political reason why the architecture of Lebbeus Woods doesn't get built. In the beginning nobody thought that these buildings were possible. Slowly, through the work of people like Peter Cook and Lebbeus Woods, there is a growing realisation that this work has a valuable contribution to make to the world of thinking architects. I think you are doing well, you are already achieving things that nobody, including architects themselves would have expected. I remember the excitement when Zaha Hadid came to my office and she showed me all her drawings and said, 'Look, they actually work in three dimensions!'

Lebbeus Woods: A year ago, it seemed like Coop Himmelblau were on the verge of a major success in terms of being able to build. But, in point of fact, now they're struggling against the loss of many of their projects for reasons that are always 'economic'. This is always the first reason given for not doing something. But the reality is that their ideas – for instance they're designing hotels – are really trying to bridge that gap between some radical approach to architecture and society as it's normally thought of in everyday life. It's a tremendous struggle because what they're telling their clients to do is to change their perception of how that social structure is supposed to work through the very geometry of space, through the way they can figure a space. If they slope a floor or open a wall in a certain way, it fundamentally changes what is expected from that kind of space. So their clients are saying, 'No, I'm sorry it's too expensive'. It's not too expensive, it simply challenges the conventions that society wants to have around it in order to feel, shall we say, secure fundamentally.

Francesco Dal Co: I would like to say something about this entire discussion of Pluralism because I think that there is a problem. I think that it is very funny that suddenly at the end of 1991 we are trying to invent a new -ism. All of the development of modern research in the field of history and criticism is best known for attempting to destroy the labels we invented. When we speak of Dadaism, of what are we speaking? If we substitute the same term Dadaism for Pluralism, it's exactly the same meaning, isn't it? We invent these labels because we are scared when we find some phenomenon which doesn't have a name. We want a name just to restrict inside the boundaries of our narrow intelligence the richness of the phenomenon. We invented the word Dadaism, which put in a prison the richness of a cultural phenomenon for which we couldn't find a name. And as we now know, names are prisons.

This is the problem and this is the by-product of another typical phenomenon of our contemporary society. We separate a critic from history; we think that the domain of the contemporary time is the domain of the critics and the past is the domain of the historians. This is completely false, there is no history without critics and there are no critics without history.

In our contemporary age, any building is subject to Pluralist judgement. In a democratic society, this is an incredible and beautiful paradox; in a democratic society there is a process which will enlarge the Pluralism of the people or institutions which are involved in deciding the destiny of a building. As a democratic society grows up, the decision of building is subject to a much more Pluralistic process of decision-making.

How are architects able to communicate with this Pluralistic society in which we live? For instance, as long as we go ahead in giving labels to the manifestation of architectural lecturers around the world, we are closing the doors to the possibility of having a real communication with this society which is expressing a growing power, conditioning the life of architecture. As long as we produce new labels and we remain closed inside our magazines, there will always be much more possibility that the people are not fundamentally educated in architecture.

Our society is completely uneducated for judging architecture. And my point is, don't we have some responsibility – all the architects of the world I mean – to create a system which allows for the possibility of a larger audience, for the users to judge on the basis of real education. We are not trained to go through our city and to perceive that architecture is the real history of the culture of humanity, not what is casually preserved in a museum. I think that the success of the Biennale demonstrates the fact that there is a need for the public to be better trained and to perceive much more what a piece of architecture is – a structure built for the need and function of human life.

Andreas Papadakis

Lebbeus Woods: Who will do this job of educating the public? The architect does it with the work that he or she does.

Kevin Rowbotham: It is absurd to assume either that the general populations in the Western hemisphere can be educated to understand architecture or that architecture can educate them. It's sentimentality, it will not happen with these political conditions of democracy. How can it happen? We're talking about millions of people.

Francesco Dal Co: I think we have a gigantic production of books and magazines in the world of architecture. We have a gigantic number of students in the school of architecture but we don't have a real system of education in architecture. I am saying that we have to fight in order to change this mentality. I'm not speaking of political transformation, I am speaking of a very slow change of mentality.

Leon Krier

Lebbeus Woods: If you really believe what you say, I think you are talking about political revolution because that's the only level on which that kind of change can happen. I don't think it will ever happen. I think the world is moving very fast and there are tremendously exciting and pressing things happening to most people outside this realm of architecture that loom much larger and more important because architects have not made architecture important in that domain. We're still too protected in our little cocoon of architectural jargon and references to really engage with people. That's why people aren't interested in architecture except for a certain cognoscenti that follow these things. By and large the world is ignorant of it and will remain ignorant, regardless of our efforts.

Ian Ritchie: I don't think it's necessarily institutions, but exhibitions which actually engage not just the architecture, but those people who are involved in the building and the physical fabric of their cities. I think that there's a way, through exhibitions, of bringing those two things together, dropping those sorts of barriers, but it's the preciousness about architecture which is the crucial barrier to ordinary people who should actually feel comfortable and part of it and begin to get the tingle of what is the art of architecture.

Roger de Grey

Martin Spring: The Pluralism that exists at the moment is to some extent quite a good state of affairs. It's democratic and it's a live-and-let-live situation, but in some senses it's disturbing, and I can well understand why architects are disturbed by it. If any style is valid, we appreciate that it has conviction. But if a student is faced with any style and has to choose any style to face his building with, we end up with wallpaper architecture. In some senses, this Pluralism has the seeds of its own destruction but how can we transcend this situation, how can we better it? Perhaps it's not through debating the validity of one style over another style, perhaps there's another way out.

Paul Koralek: I agree very strongly with nearly everything that Francesco Dal Co said. I think that when it comes to the question of training, I'm sure there's something to be done in the schools as you've just been saying and I don't think anybody would doubt the influence of some publications and so on, but surely the biggest factor is that every building that gets built is in one way or another forming people's attitudes. And the sad fact is that 99.9% of what gets built is soul-destroying and abysmal and it hardens everybody's prejudices and attitudes. I would say every time we build a building, we are trying to open people's eyes to the possibility of something new. Finally, I think people will judge on what's on the ground; that is what forms their attitudes. I think we have a huge milestone, a legacy of disaster.

Rob Krier and Rita Wolff

Rob Krier: I want to ask if anybody here, professional or not, is happy about what is happening today. The exhibition in Venice was absolutely magnificent, but is anybody happy about what was shown there?

Kevin Rowbotham: How can we be happy or not? I think it's a spurious question. I think as architects we have to confront the fact that we live in the world is as it is today, at the moment, and that is the problem we have before us.

Rob Krier: But I am in that same Pluralistic world and I am absolutely *exaspéré*; I am desperate about the situation!

Andreas Papadakis: Why are you desperate?

Rob Krier, Figure with Mask

Rob Krier: It is so confused. I have been working with students for 20 years. I have a great number of students each year but my work in the first year is destroyed by a Swiss fellow, the next year a German fellow destroys the other one, and then after five, six, seven, ten years the kids have their heads turned around in such a way that they don't understand anything!

Christopher Martin

Andreas Papadakis: I must say I am very happy about today, I think it's one of the rare times when architecture is free to take it's own direction, a direction that a wide variety of architects are taking without being afraid of either a Big Jim, or of me, or of the director of the Biennale. There are people like Lebbeus Woods here who is designing things you may not appreciate, but he is here and he is free and he is present. I can go around this room and find a variety of other architects who are like that, including you, Rob. You all build buildings that you want to and you may not have been able to do so in an earlier period when Pluralism was not around. By Pluralism I did not mean the work of a specific architect. I didn't want to press Jim, Rob, Peter Cook or anybody else to be a Pluralist architect, I use the term as a way of explaining the present, probably transient, period where architects are free to do what they want, what they think is right. Forgive me for the use of an -ism, I suppose it would have been better if I had called it Plurality.

Christopher Martin: The arguments, the debates, the thoughts that are being generated by architects and architectural writers and architectural thinkers in this country are generated, ventilated and argued, and these symposia are an attempt in a modest way to bring those things together. In their way, they are shots that are heard around the world; they are recorded, they are printed and they are distributed. They have, I believe, an enormous effect. I think the architectural community owes a great deal to Andreas Papadakis for his efforts, who believes in bringing together what he calls the primary voices, not the secondary voices, not the people who write about what other people think, but he attempts to bring together the people who do the thinking – the most important players.

Rob Krier: I would like to add one statement I forgot. I would be extremely happy to live in Gothic times, where the rules were clear, where the materials were clear; to build in brick, to build in stone. If a wall was badly constructed, it would fall down. If a church had a bad constructive section, the whole thing collapsed and with this experience, they built better and better and better. Construction is so simple and yet so silly! Never before could you make such big errors in construction as today. Without any sense of visible constructive energy, you can do everything. When I was young, I had an extremely good experience in the office of Frei Otto where we built models for the Olympic Games and when we hung some iron on it, if the model was bad, it would break so we knew we had to do it better. This is something comparable to what I was talking about with the Gothic times and how the experience can grow and be developed over years, giving a repertoire of how to build. This discussion is certainly not going on in an office of aeroplane builders, nobody would have the idea of making an aeroplane asymmetrical or Deconstructive!

Rob Krier, San Sebastian

Lebbeus Woods: Are you sure?

Botond Bognar: There is the Apollo 16 and the moon landing device, the Mighty Wolf. It's not necessarily asymmetrical, but it's kind of a fragmented form.

Rob Krier: Is a glass facade, a whole, oblique glass facade of a building, an intelligent solution for keeping the rain and the frost and the cold and the heat out of a building; is that intelligent? It's the most idiotic thing you can imagine! The Deconstructivist Libeskind designed a building for Berlin which was oblique for over 150 metres. *Bof!* A complete oblique building, coming out of the ground as a *fusil* and looking at the sky.

Rob Krier, Parvis St Germain, Amiens

Piers Gough: It was bloody exhilarating. The Egyptians built these things which are all made of stone, absolutely useless. They put people in and buried them there.

Rob Krier: The difference was that the pyramid was a symbol for something very important.

Piers Gough: Yes, but wasn't Libeskind's building a symbol?

Rob Krier: No, this is a social apartment house building.

Piers Gough: But it's a symbol of social apartment house building. Why not? It's going to be, whether we like it or not.

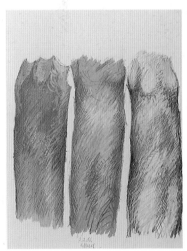

Rob Krier, sculptural objects

Paul Finch: Daniel Libeskind is probably a good reason why we need all that aircraft research, so that he can do his 150-metre spans at a 30-degree angle!

Rob Krier: Let me make a little summary of the atmosphere in our discussion this afternoon. Pluralism is certainly *une grande merde* for an architect or an artist. Pluralism is absolutely not worth talking about when we are doing our architecture, or our art or our painting. Stirling said this afternoon the only architectural problem is the quality. As a teacher I am concerned with this problem. Pluralism must be the right of everybody to talk about what he wants, paint what he wants and design in architecture what he wants to design. Every year I give my students the following exercise: design a house as honestly as possible with your friend who is an architect and designer and make for every pedestrian a reasonable, readable, understandable architectural language so that a window is a window, a door is a door and there is no confusion. The result of this can be seen in Berlin where different architects from different tendencies worked together in a way that was not so bad. The only thing as an urban designer I made them take on

board was the height and size of a building. One house was done by a Modernist, and Aldo Rossi did the house on the end. It is a normal, urban fabric, not a monumental one.

I worked on the urban reconstruction of the city centre of Amiens for over eight years. It was to be a whole city with hundreds of houses creating a tissue, built by different architects in a completely Pluralistic way, but under the dictatorship of an architect-in-chief. The notion of an architect-in-chief is one of leading an orchestra with hundreds of different violinists. We separated two days ago at Amiens because the mayor thought everybody had the freedom to make what he wanted to make, and I said no: without discipline, you cannot build up an urban tissue, it's absolutely impossible! They chose a French architect who is completely unknown in the architectural world but is famous in France for big operations at Amiens University, who builds in a style very close to that of the Centre Pompidou. High-Tech in front of a Gothic cathedral like Amiens – it turned my stomach. I had to throw the work away. This cannot be understood as a Pluralistic attitude, building a *bordel* in such a beautiful shadow!

Paul Finch: Anyway, to end this hymn to the joys of Pluralism in building, I might conclude with one personal observation in relation to labelling, criticism and how things are recorded. The problem about architectural history and why there isn't a fully satisfactory single history of architecture is because, by definition, a satisfactory history of architecture would be a satisfactory history of everything. But that in itself of course, is one reason why I think that discussions like this are worth having.

Rob Krier, Gateway Rauchstrasse, Berlin, and House Feilner, Schinkelplatz, Berlin

Lebbeus Woods and Andreas Papadakis

Rob Krier

Rob Krier, Sculpture

GEOFFREY BROADBENT
5TH VENICE BIENNALE
A PERSONAL VIEW

The Venice Biennale is an amazing, truly international jamboree of highly creative architects and students, national selectors deciding who shall be chosen to represent each country, international juries awarding the various prizes, the architectural Establishment arriving for the launch including critics who will then press their national causes with more or less chauvinism. After this it's open to the public including the gilded youth of Italy who attend in very large numbers and not-so-gilded students from other places including the UK. There are even one or two over 30s, architects and art-lovers, who actually come not so much to chatter as actually to see and think about the work.

You'd have been hard put to glean from the British Press, or some of it anyway, much about the vibrant Pluralism that permeates the Show. Some were over-chauvinistic: *our* Pavilion and not the Austrian should have won the international Prize. But we got our due recognition since Stirling and Wilford's new Shop for Electa, in the Biennale Gardens, is the very centre-piece not just of the Giardini di Castello but of the Biennale as a whole. It's a long, cool, light, immensely elegant shed; not just for browsing but for buying. No architectural book-a-holic could possibly emerge unscathed. It was splendid news too that from over 300 entries, Jeremy Dixon and Ed Jones had won the competition, for reconstructing the Piazzale Roma, that dismal bus station/car park which is as far as road vehicles penetrate onto the islands of Venice.

But the British Pavilion itself? Incredibly partisan and quite missing the point of the Biennale as a whole which was Pluralism writ very large indeed. For Britain it seems still that High Tech rules, scoring four out of six (Hopkins, Foster, Grimshaw and Rogers) against two for the Rest: (Outram and Stirling). The Rest include Stirling's career from his thesis design onwards, a touching homage but with nothing like the impact of his display, say at the Royal Academy's Foster, Rogers, Stirling Show. But to argue as did *Building Design* and the *Sunday Times* that we deserved the prize for best pavilion was just a little insular. To go on to suggest that Nick Grimshaw's literal greenhouse of an Airport – two parallel Waterloo Tunnel Terminals with a conservatory between – was sweeping all before it was, well, parochial. The test in such a show as always is how long it takes to frame up your views for unimpeded photographs? In this case no more than a second. Whereas with John Outram's drawings next door, of Blackfriars, Bracken House, Consumer Research and so on, the answer was 'nearer ten minutes'. Which is hardly surprising for what are, in terms of sheer virtuosity in presentation, quite the most stunning in the Biennale.

Of course the Establishment may still have thrilled to High Tech and there *is* a little elsewhere in the Biennale – several Australians, some Czechs, one or two of the '40 under 40' young French and some of the Germans – but it's by no means the flavour of *this* Biennale. Austria, rightly, won the overall prize because of its highly Pluralist display presented very compactly. Australia may have had more *different* kinds of buildings (Glen Murcott to Russell Hall) and so, certainly, does Italy with its 'stun 'em by numbers' range from Aulenti and Narpozzi to Ricci and Sottsass. But Austria presented almost as big a range with only eight buildings, from the Late-Modern of Wilhelm Holtzbauer, the Slick Tech of Raimund Abraham, Hans Hollein and Helmut Richter to the bent-Rationalism of Gustav Peichl, the Classical – even Biedermeier – Revival of Rob Krier and the protean Deconstructions of Coop Himmelblau and Günther Domenig.

Of course there are aspects of the Biennale's Pluralism that even this wide-ranging selection leaves out: such as the amazing timber-crafted neo-vernacular of Imre Makovecz in the Hungarian Pavilion, somewhere between neo-Gaudí and neo-Disney! Or, in the hands of his many creative colleagues, neo-Steiner, Czech Cubist, Dutch Expressionist and so on, yet all integrated into a seamless, uniquely Hungarian synthesis. This warm, welcoming and amazingly humane work from Hungary was perhaps the most inventive in the Show. No wonder they'd sold out all the books. And next to it in the catalogue is the most sterile work by far: the barely reconstructed horizontal Swiss Moderne of Herzog and de Meuron. Distinct, indeed, from Peixoto and Ohtake's towers for Sao Paolo: Vasarely sculptures writ huge in their stunning colours.

Some of our journalists, at least, caught Egypt's splendid tribute to that most humane of vernacularists, Hassan Fathy, but they missed the equivalent Greek tribute to Dimitris Pikionis, whose Acropolis paving, for instance, looks as if it's been there for 2000 years. But what, more importantly, they missed was the use of architecture as political statement, especially from the former Eastern bloc. But what, for instance, does the architecture of *glasnost* actually look like? The Union of whatever kinds of Republic they are these days present an intriguing three-part show: grandiose statements of Socialist Realism from the 20s and 30s by Iofan, Schusev and Voltsovsky; attempts at the reinstatement of human values by city refurbishment such as Vainstein's amazing (student) restoration scheme for Pskov. And, as if to declare the need to start again from where freedom and adventure were suppressed, *Constructivist* schemes, by Nekrasov, Sokhasti, Ivanchikov, Sotkinov and so on. Which, this

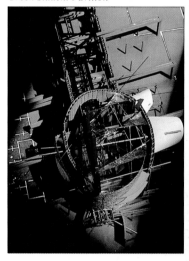
Greek Student Pavilion

Sheng-Yuan Hwang, project for the transformation of Culver City, Los Angeles

Greek students, F Avdis & M Kourniati, Urban Project

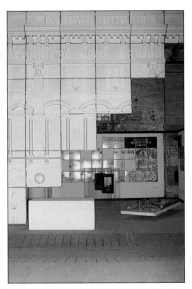

Student work from the Institute of Architecture, Moscow

Japanese student work from Waseda University and Shibuara Institute of Technology, Tokyo

being the 1990s, veered towards Deconstruction in a vertiginous display literally cascading towards the future.

The Czechs seem to have grasped more Western Slick Tech, the Poles something rather more Post-Modern, but the most touching political statements of all are the work of brave Rumanians such as Marcu. How would *you* declare the end of Ceaucescu's repressive regime, his planned destruction of those marvellous villages, his imposition of a Hitler/Speer-like axis on Bucharest and gross monuments such as the House of the People? By Deconstructionist collage of course; Ceaucescu's Classicism crumbling in homage to Lorenzetti, Vignola and so on. What better to express a country's release from such raging political *and architectural* despair. Elsewhere much planned destruction still seems to be going on, or so *BD* suggested in the Docklands-isation of Barcelona. However there are intriguing things within it and Bofill's remodelling of the airport, with its great triangular blocks of gates, offers far better access to the planes than Stansted's lumbering train-to-satellite.

BD also complained about 'deconstructed rubbish' in the Venice Prize student competition. But if any manner dominates even the adults' Biennale, it has to be Deconstruction, as one sees from Austria (Coop Himmelblau, Domenig), Czechoslovakia (Cigler, Linek and others), France (Roche), Germany (Kramm), Israel (Meker), Poland (Dom i Miasto), Rumania (Marcu and Gavris), Spain (Doménech and Tapíes), Russia (Velitchkin, Nekrasov, Vikhodstev, Ivanchikov) and above all the United States.

Where the ends of the Deconstructionist spectrum meet is with Eisenman as the most extreme of the intellectual theorists and Gehry as the most pragmatic of architectural realists. *They* steal the show, or so it seems, for most of the under 30s. Eisenman's Architecture School Extension in Cincinatti is popular enough but the crush of people around the many drawings, photographs and models of Gehry's Walt Disney Concert Hall made this, on the picture-taking scale, a building for at least half an hour. Here was richness indeed of three-dimensional thinking. One was reminded of Foster's BBC at the Royal Academy Show where there were some 80 models showing minute variations of the same basic theme. Gehry had sets of 30, 60 or so for various aspects of his building; overall form, auditorium and so on but with many more creative variations for each. The result, as it seems to be emerging, will be a veritable explosion of highly functional forms and spaces making Scharoun's Philharmonie look positively chaste, almost closer in spirit to its neighbour in Berlin, Mies' National Gallery, than to Frank Gehry's amazing *tour de deconstruction*.

So Gehry is the hero of the young, and of course it's the under-30s who will decide, internationally, not so much the going manner(s) of today as the going manners of tomorrow. It is they, rather than the national selectors, the international juries, the jet-set, critics with their various axes to grind, who'll ensure which directions architecture will take. Just as they do in dress, Pop music and so on.

John Summerson once said that he gave up being a critic because in his view the best way to comment on someone else's building was to design an alternative. In which spirit, the collected student work, from the 40-odd schools of architecture on show *is* a commentary on what more senior, published architects have been doing. This provides a far more deeply-rooted assessment of current architecture than any single critic could have written, which is encouraging because the Pluralism here is even richer than it is in the grown-ups' show. There's a little Late-Modern abstraction from Beijing, Buenos Aires, Madrid, Prague, and the ETH Zurich; some neo-High Tech from Prague and one or two hints of it from Dublin and Budapest; in the latter case a High-Tech roof over a Classical mall. As for Post-Modernism; there are hints of Mississauga from Toronto, of OMA from Delft, Helsinki and Prague; of Post-Modern Classicism from Budapest, Hanover, Ljubljana, Paris-Belleville, Prague and Venice.

There's rather more full blown, fully rendered and coloured Classicism from Barcelona, Beijing, Cracow, Hanover and Oporto. Barcelona's is accompanied by gorgeous measured drawings of Gaudí, students' reactions, no doubt, to that Minimalism which for several years now has been the 'official' language for new buildings and urban squares in Barcelona.

But of course Deconstruction that rules in the student work with hardly anything else from Auckland, Delft, Dusseldorf, the Haifa Technion, Hanover, the Mackintosh, Melbourne, Moscow, Strasbourg, the Vienna Hochschule, Weimar, the Tokyo Shibaura and Yale. And in the catalogue from Southern California although their actual display is a series of misty transparent columns! There's Deconstruction juxtaposed with other things from commendably Pluralist schools such as Budapest, Copenhagen, Dublin, Helsinki, Ljubljana, Madrid, Palermo, Santiago, Stockholm, Thessaloniki, Toronto and Venice.

Not much Deconstruction, strangely, from its birthplace, the AA, who present a stunning display of 1960-ish art, much of it conceptual but with Egashira's Tinguely-like 'Man and woman in bed' machine. But for sheer professional display though, the AA, the Mackintosh and Strasbourg undoubtedly steal the show. Here we have a right to chauvinism!

So there's very little doubt that the students, as they trudge around the huge Biennale sites, vote with their feet for Deconstruction. Which is hardly surprising since many were voting for it over their drawing boards already before they even came to Venice. Which for one thing shatters that persistent myth that students don't like drawing anymore. On the contrary they exult in drawing whether their subject matter be a single, exquisite, Ionic capital (Oporto) or a whole Deconstructed city (Vienna Hochschule).

But why this student vote for Deconstruction?

Well clearly it symbolises something; an ending of some kind. So what is it that is Deconstructed? Civilisation as we know it? Hardly, since most Deconstruction built so far has consisted of monuments to highly civilised values: Tschumi's Park, a *lawyer's* office by Coop Himmelblau, museums by Eisenman and Gehry, night clubs by Coates and Hadid. Night clubs? Civilised? Well, yes; even gilded youth need their occasional relaxation! As for the Deconstructed briefs of Eisenman, Tschumi and Libeskind, they don't exactly threaten civilised values either; on the contrary they enrich them.

Deconstruction symbolises, of course, the collapse of Modernist certainties; the 'one true way' from which any architect deviated at his or her peril. But other aspects of Pluralism symbolise that collapse too; indeed by its very nature, Pluralism itself does that. Including Post-Modern in its many guises, Classicism, that haunting Hungarian vernacular and so on. Each in itself is a potent way of moving beyond the Modern. Classicism and vernacular ignore Modernism; pretend that it never existed. Post-Modernism accepts that it did, still does, takes Modern forms and double-codes them; adds *human* references of some kind, usually from history and culture. Deconstruction too starts in the Modern but then subverts it; anticipates, as it were, the actual pragmatics of building. Simple abstract surfaces *will* deteriorate, so use crumbly surfaces to start with. Sleek, glossy structures will twist and bend so start with them twisted anyway.

The fundamental problem of Modernism as built – very different from Modernist dogma – was as Venturi insisted that its pristine forms were simply too pure for the messy realities of human use; human comfort and convenience were ignored for the sake of formal expression; for pure, simple geometry or complex and elegant structure. Such things as climate were ignored; you must have pure glass walls, perhaps turning up and into roofs (Grimshaw's airport) because any form of shading would compromise

the form. Classicism has such problems too, though to a much lesser extent; you can put one bay, two bay, three or more bay rooms behind identically spaced, sensibly sized windows, and, as Scruton argues, Classicism itself is a language that allows for a good deal of bending and distortion. Vernacular and Post-Modern both *invite* far more in the way of irregularity, fit of facade form to climate and so on. They allow different bits of the building to satisfy very different needs. Deconstruction does that too and even more so; especially such pragmatic Deconstruction as Gehry practices; if the forms don't fit the functions very well then simply bend the forms a little more.

You can see the difference at the Biennale by comparing auditoria. There are major competitions for such buildings including one for Kyoto in Japan. This has Modern to Post-Modern entries from Ishii, Isozaki, Maki, Takamatsu and Sakata all more or less constrained within elegant, blandly 'expressive' external forms. The other is a Palace for the Venice Film Festival with entries by Aymonimo, Botta, Fehn, Hentrup-Heyers-Stirling, Maki, Moneo, Nouvel and Rossi. Holl begins to break out, compromises his forms and so, somewhat rigidly, does Ungers. Their forms fit the functions a little more closely, but nothing like so closely as Gehry's. For each of Gehry's apparently wilful forms matches some aspect of function very exactly. That is Deconstruction working well; no wonder it excites the gilded young.

Model produced by students working under Hans Hollein

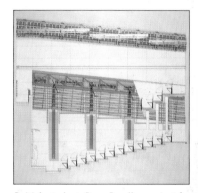

Painting by a Romanian student

British student, Ross Peedle, project for Institute of Information Technology, Edinburgh*

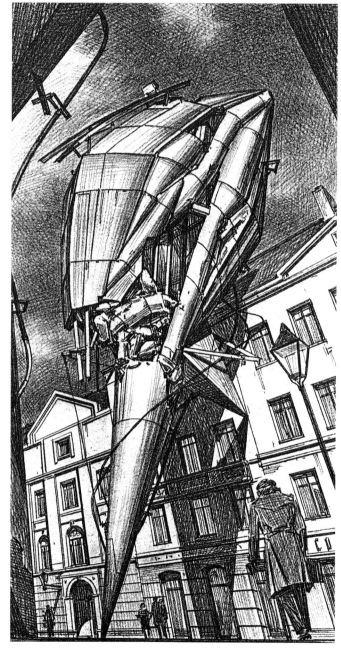

FREESPACE STRUCTURE IN PLACE

LEBBEUS WOODS

HETERARCHY OF URBAN FORM AND ARCHITECTURE

For the past three years I have studied a new type of urban pattern and form – the heterarchy – and the architectural elements that are its tissue and content. My purpose has been to envision an urban way of living that frees individuals within a community from restricting conventions of thought and action, in order to realise more fully than is presently possible to answer the question, 'What is human?' This is an answer individuals must devise for themselves, because individuals – not communities or societies are the highest and most complete embodiment of the human. So long as the individual is conditioned or controlled by conventions invented as the ethical and physical structure of society, he or she will only be able to give a partial or distorted answer in terms of the social apparatus itself and not from a deeper level of personal experience. As to why this answer is important at all, it can only be said here that based upon it (distorted or not) the entire shape and substance of human communal and private life is and always has been determined.

The projects of these past three years are *Underground Berlin* (1988), *Terra Nova* (1988), *Aerial Paris* (1989), *Berlin-Free-Zone* and *Zagreb-Free-Zone* (1991). The latter two projects are presented here, but should be seen as the outcome of these former projects and the development of ideas common to all. The ideas and factors influencing the development of these projects can be briefly summarised as follows:

The electronic revolution is breaking down the traditional boundaries between global, national, regional and even local social groups, by the indiscriminate proliferation and dissemination of information. As a result, new social groupings and new types of social groupings are now forming. These tend to be loosely-knit, continually shifting networks (heterarchics), governed by the present and changing needs of its constituents, rather than by rigid attitudes determined by traditions and enforced by fixed structures of authority (hierarchies).

Political liberalisation is growing in advanced technological societies, resulting (in its most advanced stages) in the relative autonomy of individuals within their social groups, requiring of these individuals ethical self-sufficiency and highly developed living and working skills in an ever more competitive and present-oriented economic, political and social milieu.

The revolution in science in this century has not only greatly expanded what is known, but have changed fundamentally ideas of knowledge itself. The most profound change has been in the introduction of *self-referentiality* into the philosophy (epistemology), physics (quantum theory), related fields such as neurophysiology

and cognition studies and in cybernetics, a transdisciplinary field considering relationships between mental processes and machines.

Precedents for heterarchies in architectural history are limited to certain aspects of Medieval town configurations and other vernacular town forms and architecture. However, these examples are products of hierarchial societies that lacked modern technologies. A modern example exists in the ultra-Cartesian concept of 'universal space' (Mies van der Rohe). Any other, less neutralising concept of heterarchy as applied to the design of architecture and urban form remains to be invented. Useful in this task will be reference to models of social grouping of autonomous, highly-skilled individuals, which are formed and sustained by free-choice and co-operation, such as utopian communities.

A number of my former projects have contributed conceptually to the present one with the regard to the idea of heterarchy. *Environmental Theater* (1972-74) proposes a cacophonous city of disparate parts, unified (if at all) only by fleeting individual experiences. *The Cybernetic Circus* (1973) similarly deals with circular systems of meaning within apparently disorderly urban landscapes; the idea of circus referred both to these systems and their genesis, and to a model for autonomous individuals joining together from free-choices under conditions of transient equality. *Architecture-Sculpture-Painting* (1978-79) extends the ideas of *Environmental Theater* in terms of a juxtaposition of the three traditional plastic arts. *Four Cities* (1981) derives a diversity of urban form and space from cycles in nature and primordial states of matter and energy. *A City, Sector* 1576N (1985-86) developed complex urban form and architecture from a network of interconnected, yet independent centres. *Centricity* (1987) is a city (network of cities) of interconnected, autonomous centres, disturbed by non-Euclidian, indeterminate forces, spaces and forms, the composite becoming ambiguous and complex. *Underground Berlin* (1988), proposes a community of free individuals beneath the divided city, creating an urban network based on fleeting personal experience of subtle physical forces active in the earth's planetary mass. *Terra Nova* (1988) develops the idea of a 'new nature – a second nature,' in the form of a new layer of earth reconstituted and re-formed by its inhabitants in the Korean DMZs. *Aerial Paris* (1989) extends the Underground Berlin project and its concepts, by assembling the fragments of its existential culture into kinetic structures in the sky over Paris, becoming a community of aerial performers, an aerial circus, a heterarchy of gypsy experimenters in experience. The *Berlin and Zagreb-Free-Zone* projects take this former project to the surface of

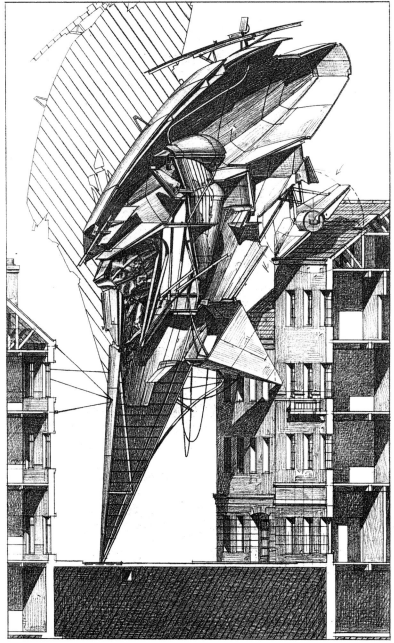

FREESPACE STRUCTURE, SECTION

two cities now undergoing profound changes and represents my first attempt in 18 years to place my ideas and work directly into contemporary urban conditions.

Architectural dynamics in the context of the preceding ideas and conditions refers to fluidity and indeterminacy in programmes for architectural design and building, as well as for habitation. Architecture and the urban field are animated in a conceptual or physical sense, achieving dynamic (rather than traditionally static) equilibrium.

Speaking for myself, the answer to 'What is human?' is a quality of becoming that is highly paradoxical if stated in terms of any existing mode of expression. This is because the human transcends limits, schemes, boundaries of every kind. Even this statement is a kind of boundary that, at the least, must be contradicted: the human can exist only within precise limits formed and reformed by the uniquely human critical intelligence. It is, in my opinion, only in the field of sensate, sensual experience – the field embraced by the idea architecture and city – that these and other-self contradictory attempts to understand and state the human can find their common, exalted basis. I have written of a new, still dreamt-of poetic science – a universcience – that will establish in the fleeting moment of the present, the architecture of a landscape suffused with the cool light of self-conscious intelligence and the radiance of transcendent love. It is this ideal alone that lures me on.

The Zagreb-Free-Zone

In order to encourage the networking of autonomous individuals, free of monumentalised institutions of culture and in the name of revitalising the true, unseen culture of Zagreb, the centre of the city is declared a Free-Zone and a network of Freespaces is established. The criteria of Freespace is as follows:
1 No *a priori* determination of use: use must be invented by those who dare to claim Freespace as their own.
2 Difficulty of occupation: the faint need not apply.
3 Absence of discernible order: hierarchy is frustrated; heterarchy is unavoidable.

Each Freespace is equipped with electronic instrumentation – nodes of energy about which the City collect. This project represents both a summation and a beginning in my work. The summation comes as a synthesis in this project of crucial ideas introduced and developed in former projects, especially those concerning the development of a new urban order – the heterarchy – and the mobile/kinetic architecture it requires. The beginning comes as a commission from the Museum of Applied Arts to realise a piece of this architecture in Zagreb, a 'freespace structure' that is a new type of building for a new way of urban living. This is the first commission I have received to build work both conceptually and tectonically entirely of my own invention, testing the strength and validity of much preceding work occurring in the form of drawings and models.

All of this has come about in a rather unexpected, even fateful way. In late 1989, word came to me through my colleague and collaborator in this project, Leo Modrein, that there was some interest in showing my work in Zagreb. The Zagreb architect Andrija Rusan, organiser of exhibitions for the Society of Architects, had seen an exhibition of my *Centricity* project in Stuttgart a year before and was interested in showing my work at the Museum of Applied Arts in Zagreb. I was very interested myself in doing this, and not simply because my 'practice' has, for the past ten years consisted largely of exhibitions, lectures and publications of my experimental projects. Central Europe has fascinated me since the early Sixties, when I first became familiar with the writings of Kafka, with the Czechoslovakian and Polish films of that era and with the peculiar, powerful East-West sensibility of this region of Europe, with its aura of harsh ideological repression and equally strong instinct for individuality. In 1977, I heard on the radio Solzhenitsyn's commencement address at Harvard in which he said that if there is to be a renaissance in Western Culture it will come from Central Europe. His vision has yet to be confirmed but it stirred my interest in that, to me, unknown and exotic part of the Western world. When the invitation came from Zagreb, a capital of the 'Southern Slavs,' at the Mediterranean end of Central Europe, I was both excited and apprehensive. The excitement was understandable, given my twenty-odd years of interest, but what was the apprehensiveness, other than that over the possible loss of my illusions?

I accepted the invitation from Zagreb but no date was fixed. In December of 1989, I was in Paris for the opening of the exhibition organised by Kristin Feireiss, 'Paris – Architecture et Utopie,' in which my *Aerial Project* was included. I travelled to and lectured at the Stadelschule in Frankfurt and the School of Architecture in Innsbruck. Zagreb, only a few hundred kilometres from there, still seemed a far-away place.

The following year was, for me, peculiar. I had finished four strong projects (in drawing and models): *Underground Berlin*, *DMZ*, the *Solo House* and *Aerial Paris*. What would – or could – come next? I worked, as usual, but without my usual focus. I made a series of drawings called *Stations*. I began a project called Island. I began a project called *Falling House* (for RIEA's Second Conference in August of 1990 on 'Anti-Gravity and Architecture'). Meanwhile, my conversations with Rusan in Zagreb continued. It was fixed that I would make an exhibition of my work in the Museum in Zagreb in late October 1990. Yet, still, I felt ambivalent about it. I became involved in making designs for a Hollywood sci-fi/horror epic. Early Fall came and went. The exhibition in Zagreb was postponed until sometime in the following Spring.

In October 1990, the impetus for a new project came.

The Frankfurt newspaper *Algemeine Zeitung* and the DAM were inspired by the political developments in Central Europe and, particularly, by the fall of the Wall between East and West Berlin. It was decided to organise an exhibition of 'the best architects in the world, prescribing new concepts for the architectural reformation of 'The New Berlin,' the centre of city reunited in the summer of 1990. The exhibition was an invitation only and included the names of those architects familiar to any reader of architectural magazines. The list of invited architects included four from New York. Mine was not among them. Nevertheless, I was determined to make a

Notes on THE CYBERNETIC CIRCUS

Freedom's just another word for nothin' left to lose. Janis Joplin

In a consumer society, the only recourse is to make one's work indigestible. Otherwise it will become the inevitable end-product of all processes of consumption: excrement.

Nothing is more indigestible than the concept of reality of freedom. Even the word is hard to swallow. It has been abused – we don't trust it. We talk around it because it is too easy to say, too difficult to achieve and sustain. In that way, it is like love, truth and beauty – they are over-used, gratuitous, drained of meaning. But if we are honest, we must admit that nearly everything today suffers this same fate. Consumer society' repetitions, exploitations, careless collaging and transpositions of images ideas, events, places, people and history, through the electronic media of mass consumption have reduced them to a common level of relative emptiness. Everything touched by these media is emptied to a greater or lesser degree of meaning and value. In other words, it is free of meaning and value, and this freedom of the material of culture from content is a most terrifying condition – utterly indigestible.

But the circus performers have always been free. They perfect their performances, their arts, sciences and skills, for no purpose, for no meaning, for no value other than the perfecting of them. What could be more meaningless than a circus act? The pointless somersault in space, the useless juggling of fantastically-shaped objects, the valueless balancing on a high wire – all hopelessly absurd.

But then freedom is absurd. Surely Camus chose his words well. His Stranger, his Sisyphus did not choose their freedom – it was their fate. Nobody in their right mind chooses freedom – it is forced upon them by greater events than their own. Nobody chooses freedom and absurdity but the circus performers. And now a whole civilisation is becoming a circus, and all its people performers in the absurd. We didn't choose it, but it happened. An entire epoch of human development – social, psychological, technological – culminates in our freedom and emptiness Now we will know that the circus performers have always known. Now we can perform for the sake of performance. We can know for the sake of knowing. We can be human for the sake of being human. Schopenhauer called it 'knowledge without interest', experience that serves no purpose other than itself – neither god nor state nor society nor even self. Now we will find out what 'human' really means.

I cannot help thinking of Kafka's Hunger Artist, whispering his final words, his raison d'etre: 'I could not find the food I liked to eat.' He was empty, his freedom unconsumed, undigested, lodged still within him, but in truth, he did not look very hard for the food he might have liked to eat – he didn't need to. He was already full with his emptiness. He was free. He was paradoxical, absurd, comic and tragic all at once. But then he was a circus performer.

And so Nietzsche comes to mind now, with his 'revaluation of all values.' The problem was, there was no revaluation at all. He who 'philosophises with a hammer, ' a smasher of idols, he who must first destroy in order to create, conducts a devaluation of all values. Do not expect 'good' news from his quarters. There will be no new values to replace the old, worn-out values. No new system will be introduced to confine and restrict as much as the old system, even though under the banner of 'improvement.' There will be no revolution turning into the same old tyranny. There will be only emptiness and freedom. Only the empty rebellion of 'we free spirits.' This is truly the death of all gods.

Neitzsche's Zarathustra was a clown par excellence. From his mouth came the words, 'You higher men, learn how to laugh. Better yet, learn to stand on your heads!' An invitation to the circus – to be in the circus – if there was one, Somewhere near the end Neitzsche wrote, '. . . better that I be a buffoon. In fact, I am a buffoon.' Free at last, he had joined the circus. The modern age was begun.

Lebbeus Woods
New York, 7 March 1991

project for the new Berlin centre because of my love for this city and my former exhibitions and projects for it while it was politically divided.

The result of my efforts, in late November of 1991, was the *Berlin-Free-Zone* project, which was rejected by the DAM for its exhibition called by then, 'Berlin Morgen' and shown in Berlin at the Aedes Galerie in February. In this project I introduced two concepts – the 'Free-Zone,' and the 'Freespace' – that were later to prove significant for my project in Zagreb. In Berlin, the Freespaces – spaces free of pre-determined purpose and meaning – were imbedded within existing buildings, the seeds of an as yet unknown culture of individual invention that might revitalise Berlin in ways the highly predictable corporate strategies and government sponsored appeals to tourism by restoration and conservation could not. The Free-Zone is the electronically woven network of such spaces, amounting to a new urban pattern, a new way of living founded on the free-exchange of self-knowledge and the inhabitation of an entirely human Nature.

In November of last year when I went off to lecture in Denmark, Germany and finally to Vienna, Zagreb was drawing closer in my thoughts. As I had made the commitment to make an exhibition in Zagreb, sometime in the Spring of this year, I began to consider what that might be. In the beginning, I knew only one thing: I did not want to bring my former projects, made for other places and times, to this City being reborn, politically and spiritually.

In the year since my conversations with Rusan had begun, great political and social changes were underway in Yugoslavia. Communism had fallen, as it had earlier in Poland, East Germany, Czechoslovakia and Hungary. A new day was dawning – but what sort of day was it? Would this country, which I had not yet visited, simply begin its race to catch-up with the West, becoming a second-rate, or at best, *nouveau* consumer culture, or would something else – unknown and exotic – emerge from the conclusion Or politics and private aspirations? One thing was sure: if I, as an American, simply presented the products of my previous work for Berlin, Paris, for *Centricity* and other places already imagined, I would be encouraging the former alternative, by offering something pre-digested for easy cultural consumption.

This was anathema to the feelings I harboured for this Central European, Slavic realm. With all my unspoken perhaps, but persistently drawn and modelled ideals for architecture and society, it was simply unacceptable that I should come to the Museum of Applied Arts in Zagreb with anything less than a project for participation in that city's transformation.

In March and early April of 1991, I prepared drawings for the *Zagreb-Free-Zone* project. They embody the Free-Zone and Freespace concepts developed in Berlin, but with significant differences.

First, the Freespace Structures in Zagreb are the streets, highly visible and aggressive. They proclaim and, in fact, contribute directly to the creation of a new state of affairs, a new set of political, social and personal conditions, at once physical and psychological a new condition of strength, but also a new vulnerability and

danger. The clarity and power of the electronic instrumentation housed in the Freespace Structures presents at the same time potential for a new elitism or new populism – all depends on the character of the individuals who occupy them, who choose to take the responsibility of the power they offer. The idiosyncratic form, space and light of each Freespace Structure provokes both seriousness and play, an ambiguity that speaks first of all of a freedom from rigid dogma, but also of an existential emptiness that makes each of us today a stranger in our own city and homeland.

Secondly, the Free-Zone itself is nothing more or less than a series of shifting centres that disturb in a human way the great pool of electromagnetic energies comprising a global field of human and natural interactions. Each Freespace structure is an element in the Free-Zone network, a point in a global matrix of communication and the exchange of personal experience and is a world-centre existing in one place and time indeterminately. The Freespace Structures are mobile. They are moved from place to place in Zagreb, from street to street, from courtyard to square, by transport helicopter; they are gypsy houses for individuals rooted only in themselves, only in the strangely social isolation of their modernity.

The drawings of the Zagreb-Free-Zone project were presented in the Museum of Arts and Crafts in Zagreb from April 22 to May 19, 1991. I attended the opening, gave a lecture and met many individuals vitally involved in the intellectual and cultural life of Zagreb today. I also began to know this city – it is cosmopolitan, complex and unpredictable, global in its sophistication, Northern in its intellectuality, yet Southern in its self-ironical *joie d'vive*.

Now the commission to build in Zagreb has come. I have returned and presented a model and drawings for a Freespace structure to be built and placed in the courtyard of the Museum, the first structure of its kind in a network – local, continental, global – that will come into being if the idea it embodies is strong enough to inspire the dedication and talents of many others.

Zagreb-Free-Zone

It is proposed that the city of Zagreb be constructed as a Free-Zone, comprised of a communications network between a series of Freespaces. This network is invested with the authority inherent in the distinctiveness of the individuals whose thoughts and actions animate and maintain it.

Each Freespace is constructed as a mobile-kinetic structure and is located and re-located in the streets, courtyards and squares of the city by transport helicopter. Each structure creates a highly particular yet ambiguous organisation of space individual invention of usefulness.

Freespace is not invested with pre-determined meaning. Strictly speaking, it is 'useless' and 'meaningless' space. The physical difficulties of occupation resulting from the eccentricity and complexity of its spatial configuration (the opposite of an easily assumed neutrality) requires occupation to be of a forceful, even adversarial kind. Freespace provokes extreme conditions, within which living and working are energetically engaged with

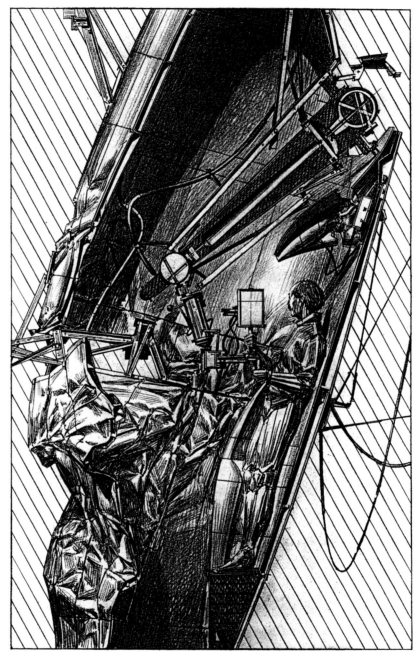

FREESPACE INTERIOR WITH SELF REFERENTIAL INSTRUMENTS

a broad range of physical and mental phenomena.

Within each Freespace are located instrument stations. These are electronic nodes containing computers and telecommunications devices for interaction with other Freespaces and locations in the world, and with other inhabitants. These stations also include instrumentation for deepening the experience by individuals of the extra-human world, the forces of wider nature at every scale, from atoms to the cosmos. In this way, individual human existence is extended into a dynamic form of human community and into nature as a whole.

In the past, it was the principal task of architecture to monumentalise the most important institutions of culture by the creation of an urban hierarchy of forms and spaces that corresponded in a physical way to embodied in the institutions themselves. Today, however, even though hierarchies of authority necessarily remain in society, a new type of order, a new system of authority has taken root in global urban culture: the heterarchy.

The heterarchy, or network, is a system of organising space, time and society comprised of autonomous, self-inventing and self-sustaining individuals and groups, the structure of which changes continually according to changing needs and conditions. Representative forms of government and free political system strongly tend towards heterarchy; free-market economies also though in both cases, these remain compromised by vestigial hierarchies of authority. Freedom of thought and action are basis for any heterarchial system, guaranteeing the autonomy of the individual and the mobility and changeability of the network itself. The individual living within a heterarchial system is characterised by the existential burdens of freedom, but also by the singular rewards of bearing them without illusion.

The emergence of heterarchial urban forms comes at this time in Western history as a result of the growing emphasis on individual existence from ancient Greek culture to the consumer culture of the present, coupled with recent technological developments such as the personal digital computer and instruments of telecommunication that simultaneously weaken the old hierarchies of authority by disseminating widely the information formerly held exclusively by them, and now make possible the relative autonomy of individual and small, flexible and dynamic special interest groups. These technological developments have been, in turn, based on revisions in fundamental understandings of nature expressed first in Relativity and Quantum Theories, then in Systems and information theories and Constructivist Cognition Theory, and most recently in Chaos Theory, whose mathematics feeds directly back into the operation of free and non-deterministic systems of the sciences and arts based on a working understanding of uncertainty, ambiguity and unpredictability in the complex heterarchies within the natural and human worlds.

The manifestation of heterarchies in the contemporary city is largely hidden, because it emerges from within spaces of individual living and working and works invisibly from there outward. These heterarchies cannot be monumentalised in the traditional sense of permanent patterns of movement, exchange and interaction even though the individual habitations part remain fixed. Instead, the heterarchies of contemporary community exist as elusive, ephemeral, continually changing patterns of free communication emanating from and received within isolated, yet distinct spaces of habitation.

BERLIN-FREE-ZONE

This project proposes the construction of a hidden city within the one now being shaped at the centre of a reunited Berlin. The hidden city is composed of a series of interior landscapes, called *freespaces,* joined only by the electronic instrumentation of speed-of-light communications, in ever-changing interactions with one another and the community of inhabitants created through the indeterminacies of dialogue. This hidden city is called a *free-zone* because it provides unlimited free access to communications and other, more esoteric networks at present reserved for the major institutions of government and business – but also because interaction and dialogue are unrestricted by conventions of use and behaviour enforced by these institutions, The *spatial forms* of free spaces render them unsuitable for conventional types of occupation, and demand instead the invention of new ways of living, even new types of activities: hence they are free in a deeper sense as well: free of pre-determined meaning and purpose. A subtle and dynamic relationship between the material realm of architecture and the dematerialised realm of electronic instrumentation is in this way established. This relationship becomes *cybernetic* in the continuous act of inventing reality.

The definition of purposes for the freespaces and the free-zone itself can only be done at present by saying what they are not, in terms of the highly deterministic language now serving the institutions seeking future prediction and the control of human activities within Berlin and the other cities. *The freespaces are useless and meaningless spaces. The free-zone is dangerous, subversive*, an anarchic *event* occurring at the very heart of the new Berlin and the new Germany. *It undermines all carefully laid plans and carefully preserved values.* The free-zone is *anti-*control, *anti-*deterministic, *anti-*institutional.

Yet the free-zone in Berlin also presents a new matrix of potentialities and possibilities. Built on the free dialogue of self-inventing individuals (not all of whom will be criminals), nurtured by their continual spontaneity and play, the free-zone is a parallel culture by definition challenging one of conformity and predictability. But it will be tolerated only so long as it can remain hidden. It will survive in the new, commercialised centre of Berlin only as long as its inhabitants maintain their wit and quickness, so long as they are free performers in a self-sustaining and secret circus, a cybernetic circus.

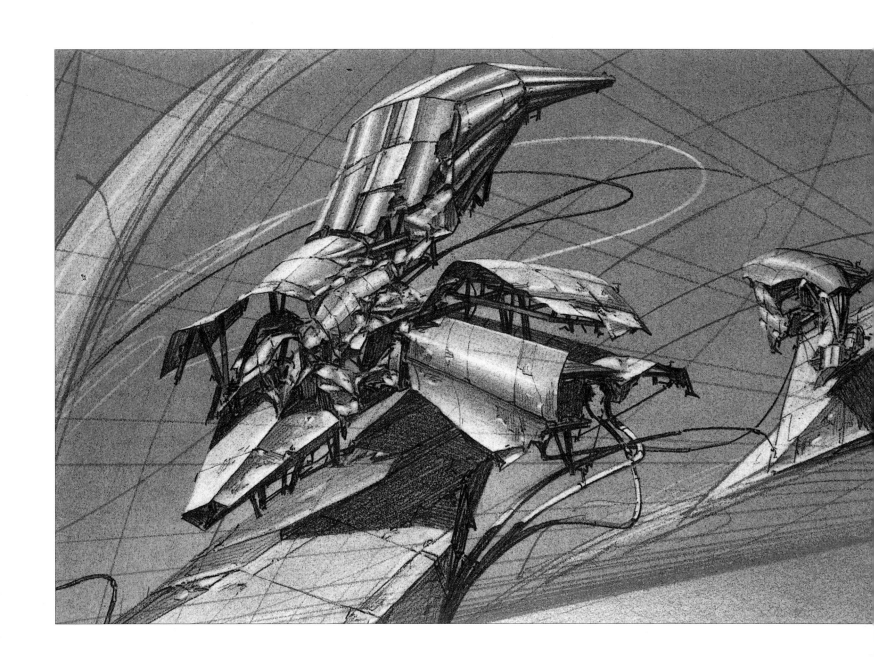

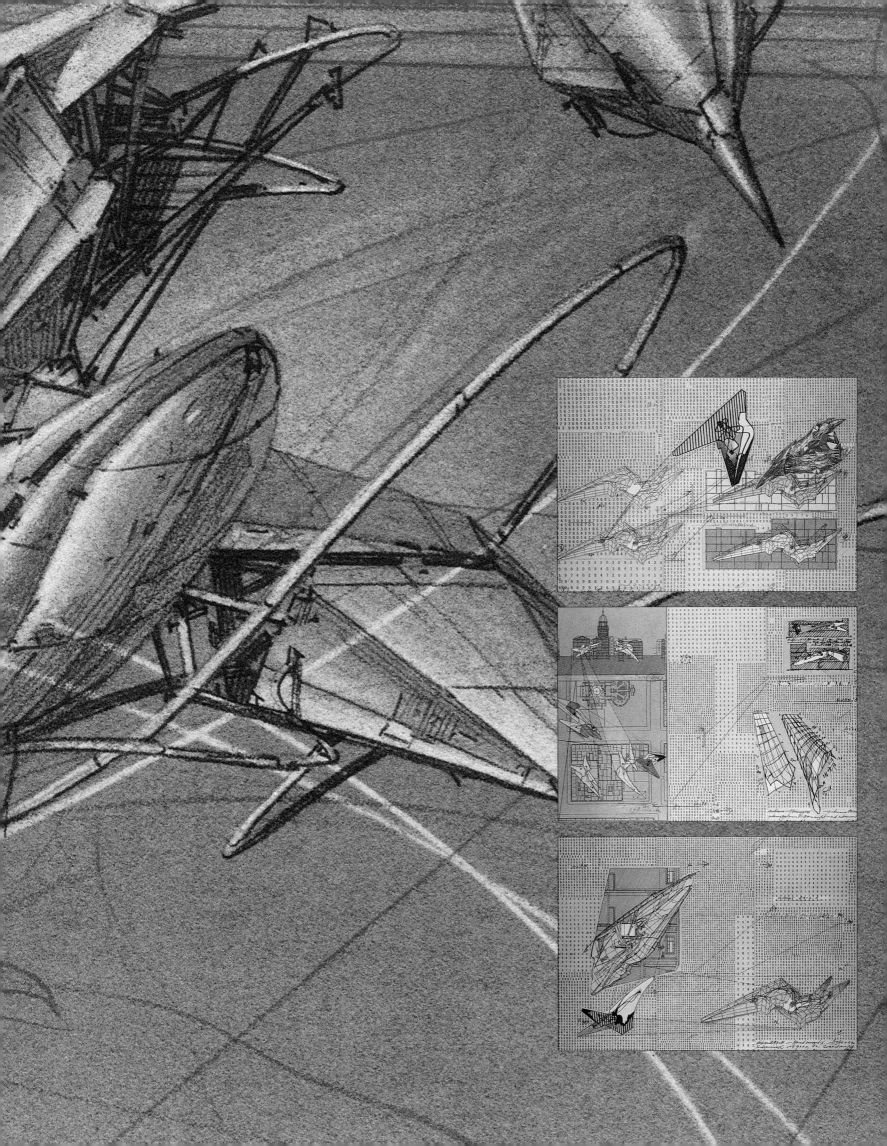

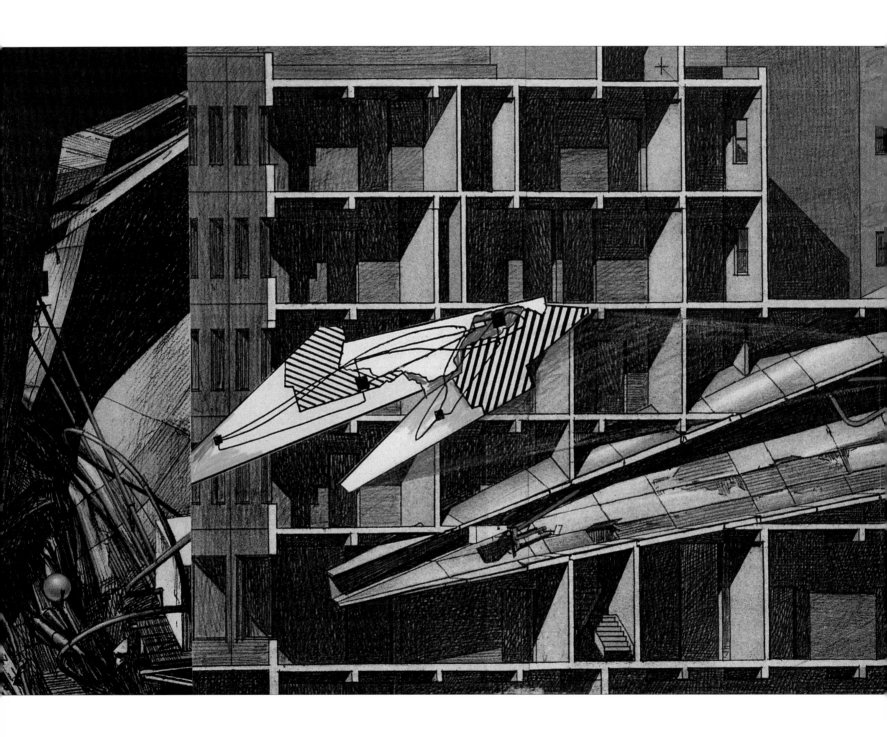

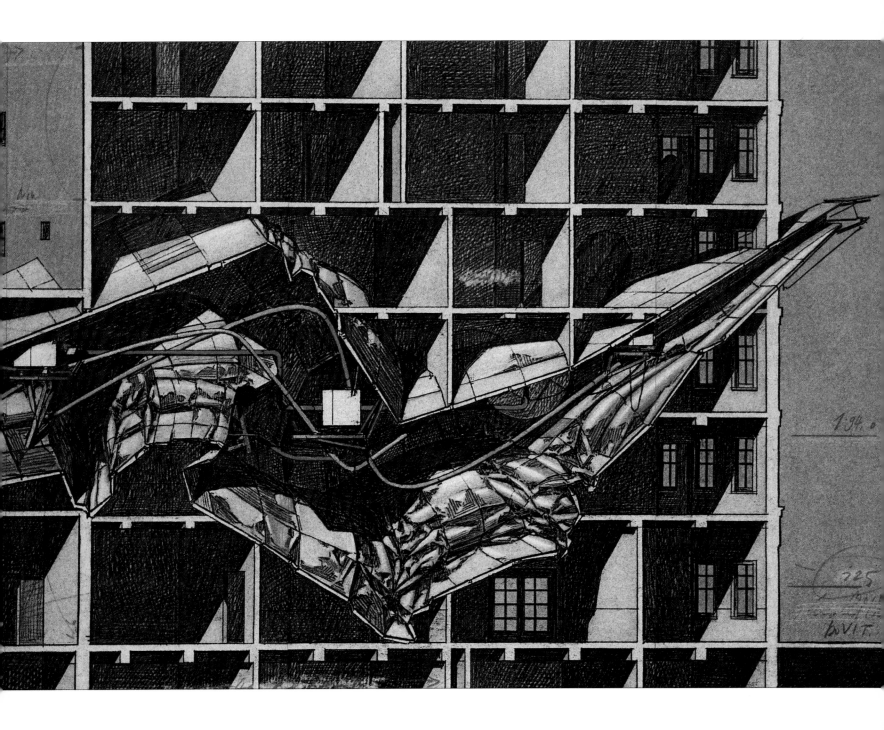

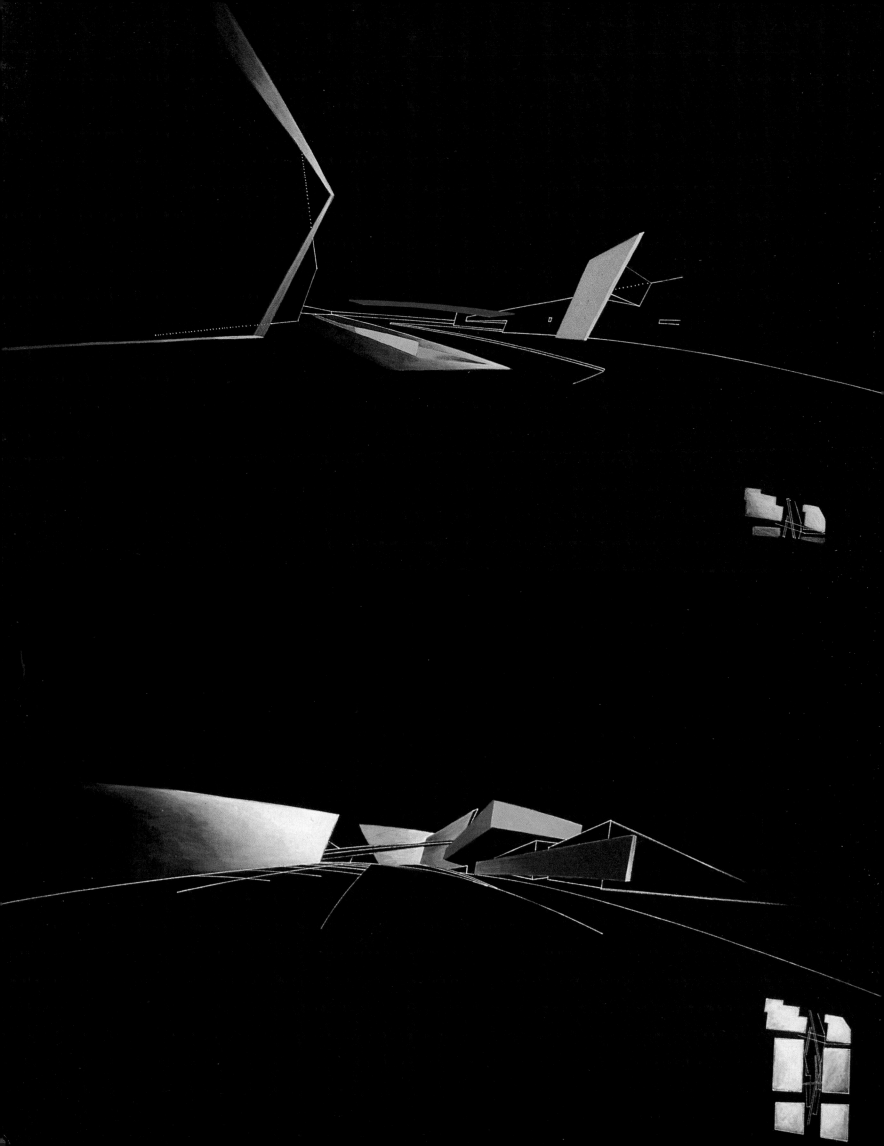

ZAHA HADID
VITRA FIRE STATION
Weil am Rheim

The project started as a commission to build a fire station in the northeast section of the vast Vitra factory complex. The brief extended to design boundary walls, a bicycle shed and other small elements.

The factory site is made of enormous sheds, with no coherent structure tying the site together. If we followed the programme strictly and put a fire station here and a bicycle shed there, it would be difficult to make sense of the whole place.

We therefore did a study of the site as a landscape as it was imperative to really understand how to make a space out of this non-space and, by that, directing the future expansion of the factory.

We concentrated on one zone, stretching from the main gate with the chair museum to the other end of the factory site where the fire station was to be located.

The fire station is designed as the edge of this 500m long zone. The zone itself becomes an artificial landscape, potentially containing more public facilities like a workers' club and sports field. Part of this landscape would be choreographic notations inscribing into the ground the ritualised fire exercises.

The proposal for the overall scheme is not the definitive delineation of the final project but proposes a dynamic pattern to allow the spaces to gradually develop. The zone is at first only defined at the one side by factory sheds while the other side is demarked provisionally by the landscape elements. Later, when sheds are erected on the other side, these elements now defining the space will become objects within a more solidly built space, like furniture in a large room. Thus the scheme sets up a scenario for forthcoming transformations of the site.

The point of departure for the fire station is a series of layered screening walls. The programme of the fire station inhabits the spaces in-between the walls which in turn are punctured and break according to the functional requirements.

The main puncture is constituted by the movement of the fire engines, perpendicular to the linear flow of the walls and the whole landscape. Sliding open the doors in one of the walls would reveal the fire trucks behind, parked under a large roof.

Captured in-between further walls, a series of linear spaces intersect, each relating to different parts of the programme.

At ground level, one beam contains the shower and changing area, interlocking with a second beam containing the fitness area, which again is linked to the outdoor fitness and barbecue garden. A stair in the intersection of the beams at ground level leads to a third which stretches between two raised terraces.

As one passes across the spaces one catches glimpses of the large red fire engines, the main focus of this landscape.

OPPOSITE & BELOW: Conceptual sketches, approach to complex

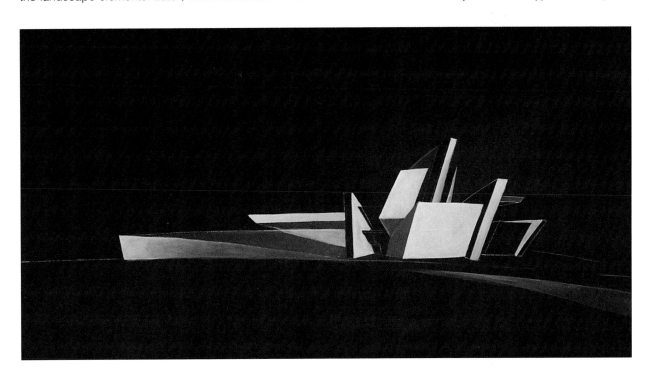

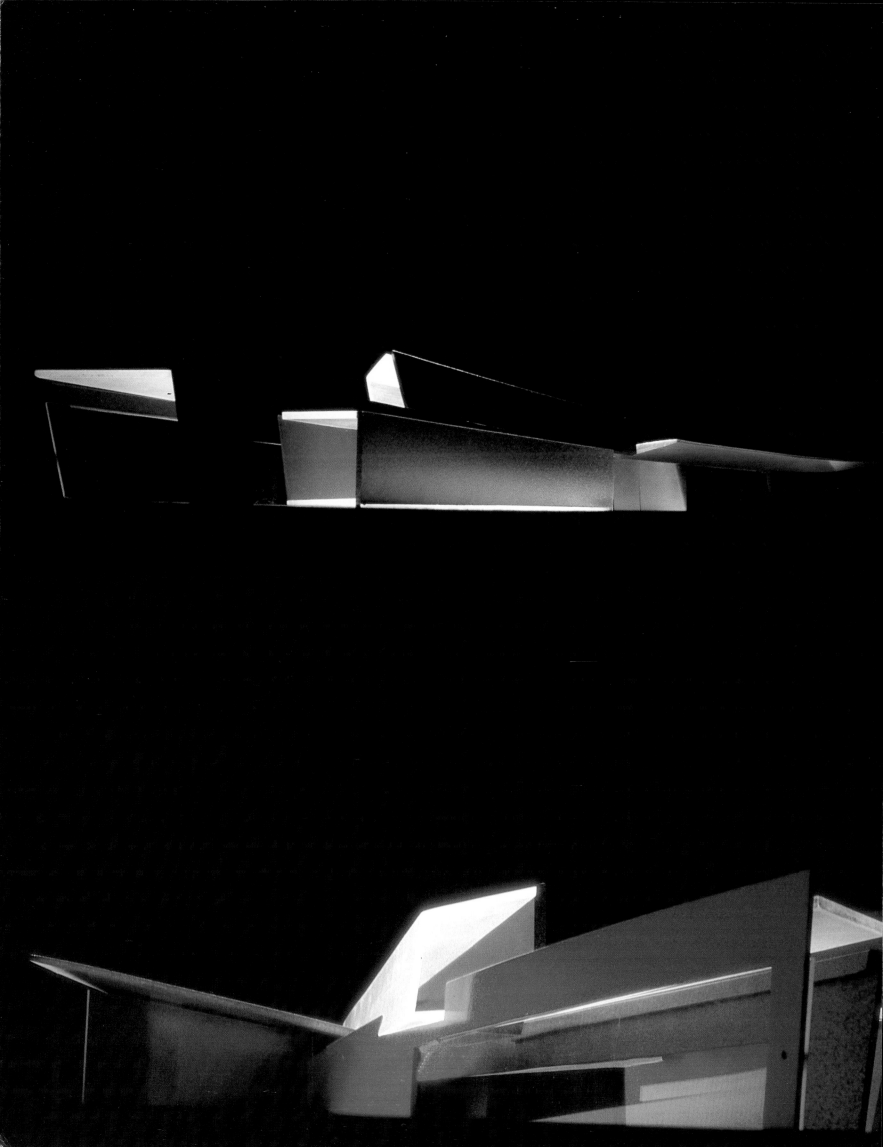

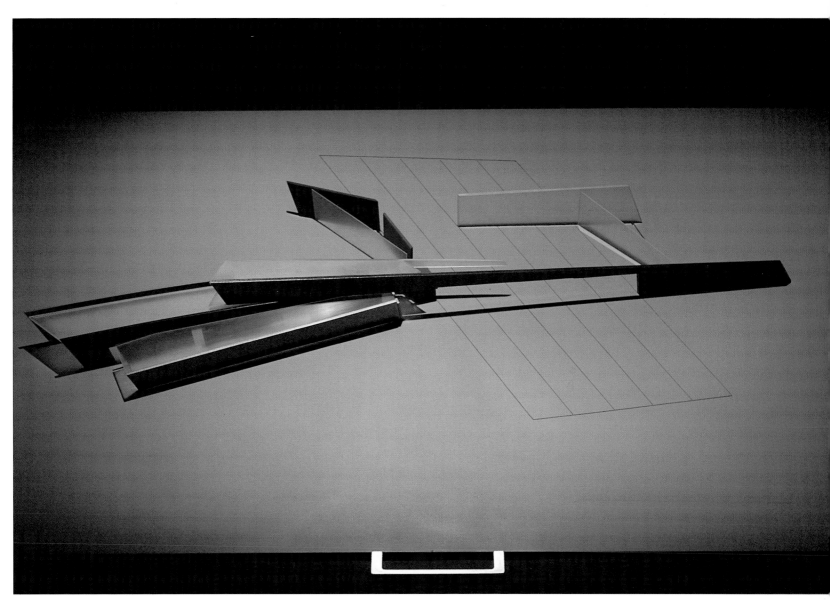

OPPOSITE, ABOVE & OVERLEAF: Model

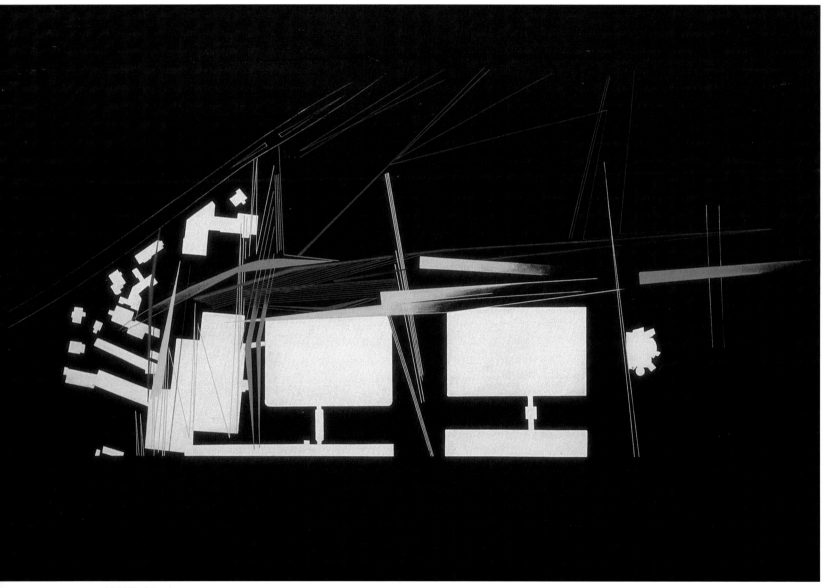

ABOVE: Site plan
OPPOSITE: Sketch of overall scheme and perspective study

MEDIA PARK, ZOLLHOF 3
Dusseldorf

The development of the site is intended to be the impetus to the transformation of the old Dusseldorf Harbour into a new enterprise zone. Redevelopments of this kind take place in many cities. So far, the potential of a new and generous urbanity relating to the scale of these former dockland areas has not been taken on.

The programme for the site, as well as for the whole area, focuses on the accommodation of the communication business and creative professions. These are to be interspersed with shops, culture and leisure facilities. A strategy had to be devised that would be exemplary for the whole harbour area.

The distinctive quality of the area is, of course, its relationship to the river. The water edge – and not the street – is looked at as the active part of the site, animated with sport and other leisure activities. For these we propose an artificial modulated landscape which is protected from the street traffic by a building which functions as a wall. Special activities are highlighted against the continuous datum of the wall.

The wall structure accommodates all the studios and offices. On its ground level are the more public related businesses (galleries and showrooms) and above, those which require more quietness. Its street side is plain and solid, while on the waterside the surface is open, partly articulated in relief, to allow for different floor depths according to needs. Where there is the need to separate a greater unit and express a certain corporate identity, then a section of the wall breaks free. The advertising agency, which breaks into a whole series of slabs, also is read as part of the wall. This cluster of slabs generates a variety of different spatial conditions inside. Where the slabs intersect a big space is carved out for conferences. Individually, the slabs provide well-lit and well-ventilated spaces for each department. The entrance lobby is at the point of intersection. The executive offices are double height spaces on the side facing the water. They have interesting visual relationships from slab to slab.

The ground behind the wall accommodates most of the public facilities (shops, restaurants, cinema) and underneath the advertising agency are deep spaces for technical studios. A big triangular plane cuts the site; it slopes against the wall and pierces through it to form another entrance to the street. From here most of the shops are accessible. For these, a system of interlocking free forms is devised underneath the slightly raised ground.

OPPOSITE & BELOW: Conceptual illustrations of overall scheme

OPPOSITE, ABOVE & OVERLEAF: Model showing internal levels

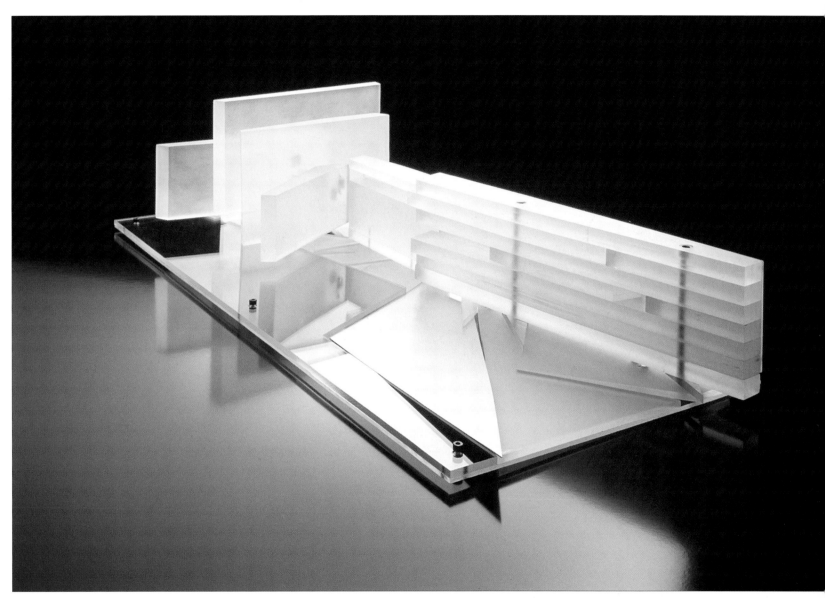

OPPOSITE: Model detail
ABOVE: Full scheme model

69

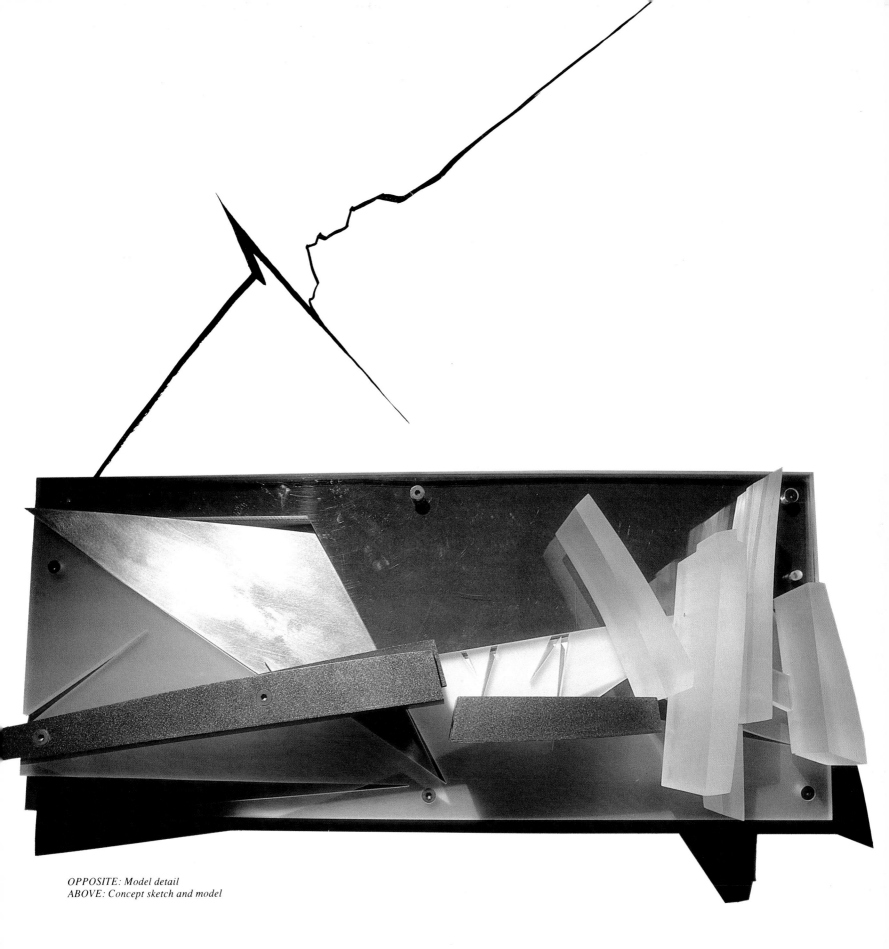

OPPOSITE: Model detail
ABOVE: Concept sketch and model

BOTOND BOGNAR
CRITICAL INTENTIONS IN PLURALISTIC JAPANESE ARCHITECTURE

For the broad spectrum of recent developments and achievements of Japanese architecture, several concrete, although interrelated and complex, reasons can be identified: the particular features and strength of the economy, the advanced systems of information and technology, the qualities of urbanism, and even the seemingly uncontrollable tendencies of contemporary consumer society.

After an age of negativity in the 1970s which was sharply critical of, and rejected the city, the 1980s, bolstered by a new economic boom affluence, and optimism, signalled the beginning of a new urban culture and with it, a rediscovery of the city by the architects.

This rediscovery also meant that Japanese architects were prompted to recognise the fact that the city as a complicated circuit of information and human desire, plus a locus of signification with floods of signs and images, was increasingly impossible to not only control, but also escape.

Japan, or rather 'Japan the city' today, more than ever, as Roland Barthes correctly observed, is an *Empire of Signs* which can only provide a context of ephemerality and volatility, and what Hajime Yatsuka called: 'An architecture floating on the sea of signs.'

One manifest symptom of this volatility is the growing number of buildings, including many well known ones,

which, after a few short years of use, like Tange's old Tokyo City Hall, or no use at all, like Takasaki's Crystal Light Building, have been demolished and replaced with something new, or are already earmarked for such destiny. Among the latter ones are, for example, Yatsuka's Tarlazzi Building and Hasegawa's Bizan Hall.

In the overall context of such an accelerated environment, a growing number of architects including Shinohara and Maki now recognise, although not necessarily endorse, the all-encompassing processes of commercialisation and the onslaught of information or media technology in contemporary Japanese society, by acknowledging their contribution to urban renewal.

As a consequence, the new architecture in Japan, more than before, is paradoxical. It is both continuous and discontinuous with the city and society, and could be characterised by a sense for both realism or more so fiction, or can it also be vision? The underlying strategies and qualities, however, are generated and conveyed in a plurality of ways and with different emphases. The more important ones are:
1 The reinterpretations of nature in relation to the city.
2 Understanding the city as topography.
3 The tendency toward a new primitivism.
4 Rediscovering the 'lightness of insubstantiality' or the city of urban nomads.

5 The application of new urban technologies, and the evolution of a new industrial vernacular.
6 Acknowledging the urban theatre or the city as fiction.
7 An increased reliance on fragmentation as *modus operandi*.
8 A pervasive spirit of experimentation.

Some of these directions are mutually exclusive, while some find themselves in close company with others, that is to say, they reveal continuities.

As for interpreting architecture in relation to nature, no architect has done more than Tadao Ando. He has, from the beginning of his career, set the irreducible phenomena of nature against the too often banal and frivolous contemporary mass culture and the megalopolis.

Yet as he does this in his recent larger projects, such as the Collezione in Tokyo and the Literature Museum in Himeji, the spatial design is more open, more layered, and perhaps more fragmented, than in the earlier, private residences, and so, these new works filter the outside world more willingly than before.

This new departure of Ando is often coupled with his long-standing although implicit interest in recreating miniature models of, should I say, 'ideal' cities within his buildings.

The courtyard arrangement of his early Sumiyoshi Row House had not only already introduced nature into architecture but also recol-

lected the notion of an 'urban' space, complete with an open-air stairway and bridge in-between the two sections of the residence.

The Galeria Akka and Collezione are more recent, larger scale and excellent representatives of Ando's urban architecture. In these new buildings, Ando, like a Calvinoesque carver, or teller of urban tales, continues to deploy elements, and even fragments, of his own imaginary city within the context of urban ephemerality. Although most of Ando's buildings remain within urban settings, several of them, like the Rokko Chapel and Church on Water, are now also found in rural or natural environments.

The critical edge of Ando's architecture, nevertheless, is by and large retained, insofar as he, in the best of his growing number of projects, continues to transform in a substantial way the surrounding landscape be it urban or natural. In other words, by way of layered walls and their interstices, carefully focused openings, and sequences of spaces Ando continues to *architecturalise* nature rather than vice-versa.

Yet, in Japan today there is another direction in which association with nature is predominant. This alternative mode of design relies on lightweight structures and thin, semi-permeable, ferrous and other materials to evoke flexible, scattered and ambiguous spaces, comparable to those experienced

in nature.

The open spaces and particularly the belvedere with its moon viewing platform in Hasegawa's House in Nerima are activated by the penetration of nature. Moreover, Hasegawa also intends to redefine 'architecture as another nature'. Therefore, she shapes her works as complex assemblages analogous to nature. The recently completed Shonandai Cultural Centre is a case in point; it seeks to elicit images of rolling hills, trees and even woods.

Hiroshi Hara's new 'architecture of modality' is somewhat similar. Turning his previously inward-oriented architectural model inside out, his aim is to make the boundaries between nature, architecture and the city as ambiguous as possible. Undulating forms, designed with highly polished aluminium plates, remind us of such natural formations as clouds, mist and foliage both outside and inside. The overlapping patterns appear as illusory scenes where the image of nature, topos, climate, and architecture is at once amorphous and ambiguous.

Yet, both Hasegawa and Hara's variations imply the process of 'naturalising architecture,' wherein architectural forms stand in proxy of nature; that is to say, 'architecture as another nature' runs the risk of turning architecture into a simulacrum of nature, and so has some inherent limitations as a critical device.

What counterbalances this process in their works is the extensive and unsentimental application of ordinary industrial materials and structures, which can render these complexes as 'poetic machines' or futuristic, man-made constructs.

On the other hand, these

PREVIOUS PAGE: Yatsuka, Tarlazzi Building, exterior detail
OPPOSITE: Tadao Ando, Collezione Building, Tokyo and Museum of Literature, Himesi
ABOVE: Itsuko Hasegawa, Shonondai Cultural Centre, Fujisawa

constructs often allude to the images of vernacular settlements, like hilltowns, as in the cases of both the Yamato International and the Shonandai Cultural Centre which is also shaped as a cluster of tiny buildings; or a small, fictive urban enclave. Toyo Ito's architecture implies a similar vision that is the quality of small, clustered villages, yet without the aspect of simulating nature. But more about Ito later. The various ways of reinterpreting nature and the city includes an understanding of them as topos. In this regard we can identify two interrelated yet eventually different directions. The first regards the existing city as a layered substratum, like a metaphorical archaeological site, and builds *out of it*, as well as over it. The Yamato International has a solid base that fills the discontinuity of the city-as-land, and builds the 'new city' over it.

In a like manner, Minoru Takeyama designed the Tokyo Port Terminal not only on reclaimed land or new topos, but also as an artificial hill with a house-like structure on it.

Riken Yamamoto, calls the 'city as topography.' Accordingly his Rotunda is designed so as to, on the one hand, comply with the rather nondescript suburban setting of Yokohama; on the other, to give birth and sustain a new kind of architecture over and above the lower 'base' section. The airy and cavernous space, with the owner's residence under the Teflon fibre tent structure, could find itself in close company with Ito's own Silver Hut.

Interpreting the city as an archaeological site gains special relevance in the Iida City Museum by Hiroshi Hara which occupies the site of the previous feudal castle.

OPPOSITE: Itsuko Hasegawa, House in Nerima
ABOVE: Toyo Ito, Historic Museum, Yatsushiro

Hara's new urban fabric, replete with wide stairways, rooftop public promenades and various scattered gazebo-like structures, is both futuristic and archaic; it is a paradoxical high-tech ruin. Two further important examples: one by Maki, who refers to a ruinous acropolis when imaging the uppermost part of his Spiral building; and Shinohara, whose TIT Centennial Hall with its flying tube concludes this line of urban topography in a curious way. It appears to reinterpret, on one level at least, Isozaki's previous vision or utopic gesture in the early 60s: the 'City in the Air', conceived as an imaginary future city over the old and ruinous one below.

If this line of understanding, the city as topography, sees the possibility of an architectural and urban renewal over and above the existing urban landscape, the other line, exemplified here by Matsunaga's Inscription House, relies on the topography of actual landscaping by embedding architecture in it. The segmented earthwork of the inscription cultivates a 'fractal landscape' as part of Matsunaga's intention to imitate or reinterpret nature.

The use of earthwork as topos is also apparent in Ito's new works in a spectacular way, particularly in his Yatsushiro Museum, where the two interpretations of topos are equally utilised. While the lower section of the building is covered by an artificial mound, the egg-shaped upper section floats above the site and the rest of the structure. The renewed interest in topography and the return to nature, on the other hand, often implies a return to the Primitive, which is a strategy to counter the overly flamboyant and

OPPOSITE: Hiroshi Hara, City Museum, Iida and Kazuo Shinohara, TIT Centennial Hall, Tokyo
ABOVE: Arata Isozaki, International Conference Centre, Kitakyushu

hedonistic tendencies of contemporary lifestyles and architecture.

In 1974 Shinohara used the earthen surface of the sloping site as the floor inside his Tanikawa residence in a manner akin to the pounded earth floor areas or *doma* in traditional residences. In this wooden house there is a continuation yet also a powerfully abstract refiguration of land, forest and nature within, and by way of architecture, with a primitive simplicity.

Toyo Ito designed his own house in Tokyo as a Silver Hut. Like Abbé Laugier's, it is a 'primitive hut', but now conceived in the modern urban environment (or jungle) of Tokyo. Instead of wood and logs, it is built of lightweight, easily available and cheap metallic materials of today. Moreover, the Silver Hut best exemplifies the new sensibilities, along which Ito now deciphers the city. He observes the fast changing urban realm as a locus where the life of people is in flux and where the physical, spatial, and formal permanence of the environment tends to lose its meaning. Accordingly Ito, similar to the philosophers Gilles Deleuze and Félix Guattari, understands contemporary city life as something approximating the lifestyles of 'nomads.' His Nomad pub was designed in two weeks as a temporary structure in 1986, and has already been demolished.

In his recent architecture Ito prefigures a potential future condition wherein the Japanese city is but a series of high-tech camps of urban nomads. Nomadic space or architecture is unwritten and undesigned, it can be traversed freely. Ito's architecture makes almost no formal statement. Comprised of thin metallic frames, aluminium

OPPOSITE: Kazunari Sakamoto, Hoshimada City, Osaka
ABOVE: Toyo Ito, Silver Hut, Tokyo

screens and other ferrous plates, plus tent structures of various configuration, the Silver Hut is penetrated and animated by natural elements such as light and wind, and in effect, actually shaped, or more precisely, formed and/or deformed by them. It is a kind of anamorphic architecture or an architecture of wind. The idea is further developed in two summer houses, the Platform #1 and #2, by one of Ito's previous associates, Kazuo Sejima. Here again fascinatingly fluid or scattered spaces are evoked by performance and come about as if by pantomime; they are almost non-existent. Sejima's works thus allude to a fluid topos, an architecture as site or locale which is generated by actions, but where action is episodic rather than sequential. As the Platform Houses demonstrate, too often this no-form, 'nomadic architecture' is comprised of little more than thin, protective roofs, like tents floating above airy, cavernous, and amorphous spaces, washed in light and shadows.

Yamamoto's 'Hamlet', a residential building with four apartments for an extended family in Tokyo, also exemplifies this well. As in many of his previous projects, he employs Teflon fibre fabric, perhaps even more extensively than before, to define an ambiguous realm of habitat in the surrounding city. Such airy, and ephemeral realms are designed in an increasing number of large public buildings. The upper structure with observation decks on top of Takeyama's neo-constructivist Tokyo Port Terminal is open to nature: wind, sunshine, and also to both the sea and the city, in between which the building intends to mediate.

One aspect is important to

OPPOSITE: Riken Yamamoto,'Hamlet' , Tokyo and Kazuo Sejima, Platform #1, Katsura
ABOVE: Kazuo Sejima, Platform #2, Kitagoma-Gun, Yamanashi

point out here, particularly in regard to Ito. He works toward the notion of urban nomad not so much as to posit literally an uprooted city. As he recognises that today no one is really without a fixed residence, he rather intends to depict an image of liberation, liberation from the marketplace and authoritarian constraint. In this respect, although their architectures represent two different modes of design, Ito's intention may coincide, even if momentarily, with Ando's goal. In Ito's and many others' designs, we witness the evolution of another new paradigm of Japanese architecture which, as opposed to Ando's works of substantiality, is characterised by lightness, permeability, fluidity of space, a feeling for temporality and an almost 'immaterial evocation of building'. This paradigm is often closely related to a new interpretation and application of technology, different from the idealised one, upon which modernism was built.

The reliance on new technologies in a widening spectrum of contemporary Japanese architecture, has begun to impart a new technological landscape. It has led to both a new industrial vernacular, as exemplified here by Hasegawa's House in Oyamadai, and has yielded to increasingly difficult, highly elaborated and heavy personal styles and frustrated monuments in search of meaning as in the case of Shin Takamatsu.

The new urban technology is primarily an architectural software technology, that ranges between a straightforward simplicity, and a highly sophisticated craftsmanship, often with manneristic overdetailing, but in both cases with a strong appeal to the senses or sensuality. This technology with its

OPPOSITE & ABOVE: Mioru Takeyama, Port Terminal, Tokyo

85

fuzzy logic, is both derived from and responds to the existing urban conditions that are predicated on the Japanese feel for not only reality, but also fiction.

The new technological landscape therefore is the outcome of contradictory conditions and partial interventions, while producing heterogeneities rather than the homogeneity of an *a priori* order.

The new 'architectural machine' and the landscape its technology produces is thus non-structural, or more precisely, post-structuralist and as such, non-hierarchical. It results in an architecture of and by 'autonomous' parts, and further, in a 'fragmented landscape,' as in the case of Ito's Yatsushiro Museum for instance.

In many recent Japanese works there appears to be no formal statement; yet they reveal an implicit intention to break the unity of form. In respect to fragmenting form by way of a new technology, Kazuo Shinohara, Fumihiko Maki, and Arata Isozaki should be also mentioned.

Shinohara's House in Yokohama is, more than any time before in his architecture, an agglomeration of parts, like parts in a peculiar 'zero degree machine' as he calls it. Shinohara's inspiration comes from the latest technological advancements of our times such as the moon-landing module or F-14 fighter plane which exhibit forms of extreme complexity, yet are devoid of the streamlined formal synthesis the pioneers of the Modern Movement were striving for.

The various individual forms and volumes of the house, all corresponding to different functions, are joined abruptly. By way of this abrupt, by no means unconditional, mode of assembling, Shinohara, like

OPPOSITE: Toyo Ito, Tower of Wind, Yokohama
ABOVE: Itsuko Hasegawa, House at Oyamadai, Tokyo

many of his contemporaries, has achieved a new *sachlich* or objectivity in design, as well as a formal integration without synthesis.

Fragmentation however does not mean that there are no structural or tectonic considerations in shaping the new architecture and technological landscape. Maki's architecture is a case in point. The Municipal Gymnasium in Fujisawa has been designed with an engineering bravura. Yet Maki seems to have done everything to break the continuity and unity of form. This is particularly evident when the building is compared to another masterpiece of 20 years earlier, that is Tange's Tokyo Olympic Gymnasia. The unique articulation of structural and formal elements and treatment of surfaces in Maki's project assure that every new vantage point reveals a new silhouette, a new facade, (or face even) and a new hallucinatory image. These images continuously fluctuate between a wide range of traditional and futuristic or high-tech references.

Another example of such engineering and structural considerations is Shinohara's TIT Centennial Hall. Shinohara has, for quite some time, been pursuing the concept of 'progressive anarchy' as the focus of his design, in parallel with his intention to assemble 'zero-degree machines.' The TIT Centennial Hall admittedly draws from the chaotic energy, ways and means of perception, as well as the a-logic of its urban nexus; but by way of its appeal to a new machine aesthetics or new-tech, it also opposes the uncontrolled accesses of the existing city, especially the all too often trivialising modes of signification and representation of the con-

OPPOSITE: *Fumihiko Maki, Municipal Gym, Tokyo and Municipal Gym, Fujisawa*
ABOVE: *Fumihiko Maki, Municipal Gym, Tokyo*

sumerist city. Therefore, the new urban technology, as a mode of dissimilation, can also manifest an effective criticism of bourgeois representation and representational architecture.

Rather than reusing a formal tradition, Maki often responds to the layered, collage-like quality of the heterogeneous Japanese city by articulating his buildings, like the Spiral, with sequentially layered spaces that, similar to traditional architecture, involves the intricate arrangement of surfaces and, as in the Tepia Science Pavilion, the use of various screens, and in so doing, the conjuring up of a phenomenological depth. Accordingly, building envelopes of Maki's works have become gradually 'detached' from the tectonic body and, acquiring a certain sign quality, freely manipulated. In this process we may discover the traces of scenography forwarded by an increasingly sophisticated technology, so that we are at a point of intersection at which the interpretation and use of technology moves in a different direction.

This intersection has already been foreshadowed in one of Isozaki's early visionary urban projects in which both new technology and an old, ruinous urban landscape play important roles. It is the sign of an urban theatre – or is it a fiction created by technology? But it is the Tsukuba Centre Building where Isozaki first actually realised such a stage set for the urban theatre. The line of theatricality continues to dominate much of his present architecture as well, although without the witty irony that imbued his previous work until the early 80s. Isozaki's new International Convention Centre at

OPPOSITE: Kazuo Shinohara, TIT Centennial Hall, Tokyo
ABOVE: Fumihiko Maki, Tepia Science Pavilion, Tokyo

the port of Kitakyushu has been conceived as a metaphor of a ship, perhaps a wrecked ship, whose fragments seem to float on the sea – both real and metaphoric.

One of Isozaki's disciples, Hajime Yatsuka, investigates similar issues. His Tarlazzi Building is a playful collection of architectural fragments engaged in an elegant dance in front of the black surface of the large rear wall or facade. In this play the protagonists are the fragmented signs or the ruins of technological modernity. Although not yet fully independent of its mode of building or construction, it is an architecture that floats 'on a sea of signs', revealing a curious co-vibration with both modernism and the urban theatre of Tokyo which, indeed, appears to be nothing but signs.

Eventually, technology too can be rendered as merely a sign. In Shin Takamatsu's Week Building it is hardly more than a sign of itself: technology rendered as decorum. It is what may be called 'dead-tech'. In the case of his Kirin Plaza in Osaka, technology is both an *appliqué* on the facade and a computer controlled system of electric signs. The building is both everyone's daydream and nightmare at the same time; it is a cybernetic vision, an urban 'desiring machine,' a fiction by technology; and as such, and like the Japanese city at large, it is also superficial. It is a delirious urban theatre, a stage set, wherein, as in Takamatsu's many other works, the Solaris, for example, the ephemeral and the concrete; the metaphysical and the banal; progress and decadence; and further, both reality and fiction are equally signified in a state of despair. Although

OPPOSITE & ABOVE: Shin Takamatsu, Syntax Building, Kyoto

Takamatsu's case is unique in its singular extremity, for many Japanese architects, reality and fiction appear to be one and the same thing. This understanding however is not entirely new. The qualities of a 'floating world' did imbue Japanese life and architecture almost as much in the past as they do at present.

The Japanese have always preferred to apprehend things as events rather than substance. Nevertheless, this is an aspect of Japanese architecture and urbanism which is the most vulnerable to the exploitation of the marketplace. Today, the Oriental Japanese attitude of 'all things must pass' can easily be interpreted as 'all things must sell'. And with this, the circle of events seems to be completed and the paradoxical circuits closed. In critical and affirmative architectures the borderline is rendered infinitely thin and almost invisible. And it is the predicament of this borderline condition wherein any resistive or critical practice can hope to operate today, by way of an extraordinary act of balancing on – what Yatsuka called – a 'tightrope over the abyss.'

 OPPOSITE & ABOVE: Shin Takamatsu, Solaris Building, Nishinomiya
OVERLEAF: Shin Takamatsu, Kirin Plaza Building, Osaka